SKEUL AN TAVAS

*A Cornish language coursebook for adults
in the Standard Written Form
with Traditional Graphs*

Second dyllans • Second Edition

Scrifys gans
Ray Chubb

Lymnys gans
Nigel Roberts

Agan Tavas
2010

Dyllys gans Agan Tavas, Gordon Villa, Sunnyvale Road, Portreath, Redruth, TR16 4NE, Kernow / Cornwall, UK. *www.agantavas.com.*

Penscriforyon: Michael Everson ha Nicholas Williams

Second dyllans 2010. Daspryntys gans ewnansow Genver 2011.
Second edition 2010. Reprinted with corrections January 2011.

Y kevyr covath rolyans rag an lyver-ma dhyworth an Lyverva Vretennek.
A catalogue record for this book is available from the British Library.

ISBN-10 1-901409-12-0
ISBN-13 978-1-901409-12-3

Olsettys yn Warnock Pro hag **Anzeigen Grotesk** gans Michael Everson.

Lymnans: Nigel Roberts.

Cudhlen: Michael Everson. Skeusen: Alexander Popov.

Pryntys gans LightningSource.

Foreword

The Standard Written Form for the Cornish Language, intended for use in education and public life, was published in June 2008. This coursebook has been produced by Agan Tavas to meet the needs of those learning under the structure of the Languages Ladder programme of the UK Department for Children, Schools and Families. Unlike some other coursebooks, this book teaches Cornish in a "can-do" way, and does not expect students to know the finer points of Cornish grammar from the beginning. That is not to say that grammar can be avoided. Cornish is a Celtic language, like Welsh and Manx, and the rules governing its inflection and syntax are very different from those of English and such rules have to be learned. The course starts with the basics—all presented in a friendly and accessible way.

This course is aimed at the Breakthrough level of the Languages Ladder. This consists of three stages and *Skeul an Tavas* is divided into three parts, each corresponding to one of those stages. The book is intended for internal teacher assessment in the stages leading to Breakthrough, but the whole specification required by a student to take the external assessment at Breakthrough level is covered in this book.

The book contains many practical examples of natural Cornish. Students can practise adding to what they have learned by constructing further examples with the use of a dictionary. *Skeul an Tavas* contains a complete glossary of all the Cornish words in the book. The illustrations will help students to learn the meaning of many Cornish words without reference to English. *Skeul an Tavas* will help any student to acquire Cornish as a spoken language for everyday use. Therefore most will be gained from this book if students endeavour to work out the meaning of words from the pictures themselves, consulting the word list at the back only as a last resort.

The spelling used in this book follows the rules of the Standard Written Form agreed by the Cornish Language Partnership for use in education and public life. It employs the Traditional Graphs recommended for writers who wish to use more historically-based spelling. Agan Tavas believes that adults will wish to learn a form of Cornish that is close to the historical texts, thus making the spelling of those texts and also of Cornish place names and surnames, more familiar. The rules of the Standard Written Form make it clear that, as far as examinations are concerned, students may use either Main or Traditional Graphs in their answers.

Agan Tavas has worked together with Evertype to produce *Skeul an Tavas* in three editions. Agan Tavas has published two versions, one in the Standard Written Form with Traditional Graphs (SWF/T, with a green cover, for those who intend to use the book in adult education classes) and the other in the Standard Written Form with non-traditional (so-called "Main Form") Graphs (SWF/M, with an orange cover, for those who intend to use this book in schools or in public administration). Evertype has published the Standard Cornish (KS) version (with a blue cover, for those who wish to use a more thoroughly researched and phonetically accurate orthography).

Both Agan Tavas and Evertype would like to acknowledge the assistance of Jenefer Lowe and Pol Hodge of the Cornish Language Partnership (MAGA), as well as that of Daniel Prohaska, in the preparation of this revised edition.

Ray Chubb
Portreath

Rol an Lyver
Table of Contents

Rann Onen
Part One

At the end of part one of this book you should be able to:

- Understand a few familiar spoken words and phrases
- Recognize and read out a few familiar words and phrases
- Say and repeat single words and short simple phrases
- Write or copy simple words correctly

Dyscas Onen
Lesson One

Cornish like all the other Celtic languages (Welsh, Breton, Irish, Scottish Gaelic, and Manx), has a feature which is known as *initial consonant mutation*. That is, the first letters of words are changed depending upon what comes before. Learning about mutation in Cornish at an early stage can avoid confusion later on.

The first mutation that we learn about is known as the *Second State*, or Lenition. The *First State* is the basic word before any change is made to it.

The definite article, **an** 'the', causes 2nd state mutation when it is followed by a feminine noun.

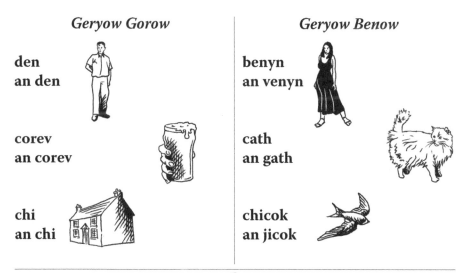

Geryow Gorow	*Geryow Benow*
den an den	benyn an venyn
corev an corev	cath an gath
chi an chi	chicok an jicok

Geryow Gorow		*Geryow Benow*	
dehen an dehen		davas an dhavas	
glaw an glaw		garr an arr	
gool an gool		goodh an woodh	
gwely an gwely		gwelen an welen	
gwri an gwri		gwragh an wragh	
maw an maw		mowes an vowes	
pons an pons		pluven an bluven	
qwilkyn an qwilkyn		qweth an gweth	
to an to		tesen an desen	

Practis Onen
Exercise One

Using the examples above, write **an** before the following feminine nouns: **derowen** 'oak tree', **canstel** 'basket', **gwlas** 'country', **Gorsedh** 'the Cornish Gorsedd', **gwedren** 'glass, tumbler', **gwreg** 'wife', **melin** 'mill', **padel** 'pan, saucepan', **tre** 'farm, home, town', **gwedhen** 'tree'.

When you have done this try and memorize all the words that you have learned so far.

In Cornish the adjective almost always follows the noun; so we say the equivalent of 'a dog black' not 'a black dog', which in Cornish is **ki du**. Note that in Cornish we do not use the equivalent of English 'a' or 'an', the indefinite article. In Cornish, we manage quite well without it!

When a feminine noun is followed by an adjective the adjective is given Second State mutation as we have learned above.

Ensamplys:

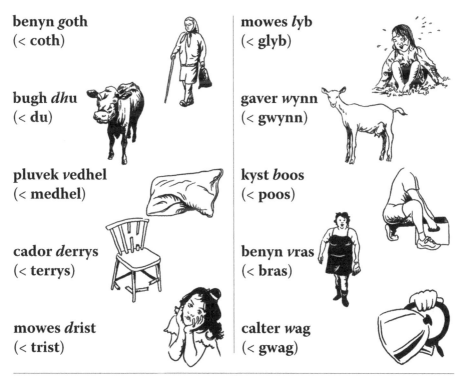

benyn goth
(< **coth**)

bugh dhu
(< **du**)

pluvek vedhel
(< **medhel**)

cador derrys
(< **terrys**)

mowes drist
(< **trist**)

mowes lyb
(< **glyb**)

gaver wynn
(< **gwynn**)

kyst boos
(< **poos**)

benyn vras
(< **bras**)

calter wag
(< **gwag**)

Questions and Answers

We now learn to make simple statements and ask questions and answers about the words that we have learned:

'This':
Hemm yw den. 'This is a man.'
Homm yw benyn. 'This is a woman.'
Yw hemma ki? 'Is this a dog?'
Yw homma davas? 'Is this a sheep?'
Yw, den yw hemma. 'Yes, this is a man.'
Yw, benyn yw homma. 'Yes, this is a woman.'
Nag yw, nyns yw homma davas. 'No, this is not a sheep.'

'That':
Henn yw den. 'That is a man.'
Honn yw davas. 'That is a sheep.'
Yw henna gwely? 'Is that a bed?'
Yw honna calter? 'Is that a kettle?'

'What?'
Pyth yw henna? 'What is that?'
Henn yw pons. 'That is a bridge.'
Pyth yw homma? 'What is this?'
Homm yw kyst. 'This is a box.'

Sometimes a Second State mutation is pronounced but with no change in spelling. The sound of the letter **f** can change to **v** and the sound of the letter **s** can change to **z**.

fordh
an fordh
(an vordh)

sarf
an sarf
(an zarf)

Practis Dew
Exercise Two

Write or speak replies in the forms shown above so that your answers
fit the form of the questions

Yw hemma gwely? . . . .

Yw homma sarf? . . . .

Yw henna qwilkyn? . . . .

Yw honna calter? . . . .

Pyth yw hemma? . . . .

Pyth yw honna? . . . .

Yw hemma maw? . . . .

Yw homma benyn? . . . .

Yw henna pellwolok? . . . .

Yw honna davas? . . . .

Pyth yw henna? . . . .

Pyth yw homma? . . . .

Yw hemma gwri? . . . .

Yw homma kyst? . . . .

Yw henna gaver? . . . .

Yw honna pluven? . . . .

Pyth yw hemma? . . . .

Pyth yw honna? . . . .

Dyscas Dew
Lesson Two

In this lesson we learn how to ask and reply about what something is like. We will learn some adjectives, and about some ways of asking questions. First of all we need to know how to say; 'this house' 'that dog', and so on in Cornish. To say 'this' we put **an** before the word and **-ma** after it. To say 'that' we put **an** before the word and **-na** after it.

Yw an pysk-ma byhan po bras?
Is this fish little or big?

Pysk byhan yw. Byhan yw.
It's a little fish. It's small.

Yw an pysk-na byhan po bras?
Is that fish little or big?

Pysk bras yw. Bras yw.
It's a big fish. It's big.

Practis Tri
Exercise Three

Answer the questions below chosing an appropriate adjective. Remember to use the correct mutation!

New words: **carrek** 'rock', **du** 'black', **glyb** 'wet', **gwag** 'empty', **gwynn** 'white', **leun** 'full', **lowen** 'happy', **poos** 'heavy', **pedrek** 'square', **pel** 'ball', **rond** 'round', **rudh** 'red', **saw** 'intact, whole', **scav** 'light', **segh** 'dry', **tanow** 'thin', **terrys** 'broken', **tew** 'thick', **trist** 'sad'.

Gorow

Yw an daras-ma
gwynn po du?

. . . .

Yw an daras-ma
gwynn po du?

. . . .

Yw an lyver-ma
tew po tanow?

. . . .

Yw an flogh-ma
lowen po trist?

. . . .

Yw an treys-ma
glyb po segh?

. . . .

Benow

Yw an fenester-ma
saw po terrys?

. . . .

Yw an balores-ma
du po rudh?

. . . .

Yw an wedren-ma
leun po gwag?

. . . .

Yw an garrek-ma
poos po scav?

. . . .

Yw an bel-ma
rond po pedrek?

. . . .

Kewer / an Gewer
Weather / the Weather

Another way to ask what something is like is with the word **fatel** 'how'.
We will now use **fatel** to talk about the weather in the past, present,
and future. Note also that to say 'yes' and 'no' in Cornish the reply has
to agree with the form of the question. For example:

O an gewer tomm? O, tomm o.
Was the weather hot? Yes, it was hot.
(Literally 'Was the weather hot? [It] was, hot [it] was.')

A vydh an gewer tomm? Na vydh, ny vydh tomm.
Will the weather be hot? No, it will not be hot.
(Literally 'Will-be the weather hot? [It] not will-be, hot [it] will-be.')

A vydh an gewer yeyn? Bydh, yeyn vydh.
Will the weather be cold? Yes, it will be cold.

11

de	hedhyw	avorow
yesterday	today	tomorrow

Ensamplys:

Fatel o an gewer de?
Tomm o an gewer de.
Tomm o.

Fatel yw an gewer hedhyw?
Gwynsek yw an gewer hedhyw.
Gwynsek yw.

Fatel vydh an gewer avorow?
Yeyn vydh an gewer avorow.
Yeyn vydh.

O an gewer de tomm?
Nag o, nyns o tomm.
Comolek o.

A vydh glyb an gewer avorow?
Na vydh, howlek vydh.

A vydh tomm an gewer avorow?
Bydh, tomm vydh.

Practis Peswar
Exercise Four

New words: **segh** 'dry', **clor** 'mild', **howlek** 'sunny', **brav** 'fine'.
Answer the following questions:

**Fatel yw an gewer
hedhyw?**

. . . .

Fatel o an gewer de?

. . . .

**Fatel vydh an gewer
avorow?**

. . . .

**Yw an gewer
hedhyw howlek?**

. . . .

When you have completed this try discussing the weather in the
present, past, and future with others in the class.

Asking each other how we are

First of all it would be useful to know how to say 'hello' and 'good-
bye' in Cornish. Most speakers say **dedh da**, but if you want to show
how clever you are, you can use a form found in historical Cornish
which is **durda dhis**. 'Good-bye' is **Duw genes**.

To ask how someone is we say **fatla genes?** 'how is it with you?' The word **fatla** is just another form of **fatel**. We reply by placing the describing part first and follow this by **ov vy** 'I am' (literally 'am I'); this may be shortened to **ov**.

Ensamplow:

Fatla genes?	**Tomm ov vy.**	I am hot.
Fatla genes?	**Yn ta ov vy.**	I am well.
Fatla genes?	**Da lowr ov vy.**	I am well enough.
Fatla genes?	**Sqwith ov vy.**	I am tired.
Fatla genes?	**Lowen ov vy.**	I am happy.
Fatla genes?	**Trist ov vy.**	I am sad.
Fatla genes?	**Sad ov vy.**	I am serious.
Fatla genes?	**Yagh ov vy.**	I am in good health.
Fatla genes?	**Drog ov vy.**	I am naughty (or bad).

Tamsyn and Wella meet in the street and have the following conversation. *New words*: **mes** 'but', **y'n** 'in the'. Adding **tejy** 'you' makes **genes** 'with you' stronger:

Tamsyn	**Dedh da, Wella.**
Wella	**Durda dhis, Tamsyn, fatla genes?**
Tamsyn	**Da lowr ov vy, mes sqwith ov. Fatla genes tejy?**
Wella	**Lowen ov vy. An gewer yw tomm hedhyw.**
Tamsyn	**Yw, mes avorow an gewer a vydh glyb.**
Wella	**Henna a vydh drog.**
Tamsyn	**Bydh. Yw pel an dra-na y'n fordh?**
Wella	**Yw, pel vyhan yw.**
Tamsyn	**Duw genes, Wella.**
Wella	**Duw genes, Tamsyn.**

Try this among each other; first of all take parts and read the above conversation aloud. After this make up your own typical conversations for two people who meet in the street based on what you have learned so far, and practise them with each other. Try and get to the stage where you can hold the conversation without reading notes.

Dyscas Tri
Lesson Three

In this lesson we look at the verb **bos** 'to be' ('am', 'are', 'is'). The verb is shown below for all persons in the present tense. Note that Cornish, unlike English in most parts of England, has not lost the second person singular form, 'thou'. The subject comes before the verb in these examples. The word **ha** 'and' becomes **hag** before **a, e, eu, i, o, u,** and **y** (when used as a vowel).

Den *ov vy.*

 Den ha benyn *on ni.*

Benyn *os ta.*

Maw ha mowes *owgh whi.*

Maw *yw ev.*

Mowes *yw hi.*

Mowes ha maw *yns i.*

The phrases above use the personal form of the verb, which is used when the subject is the first word. When the subject follows the verb, we can say the same thing using the third person form of the verb impersonally.

my yw **den**   *ni yw* **den ha benyn**

ty yw **benyn**   *whi yw* **mowes ha maw**

ev yw **maw**

hi yw **mowes**   *i yw* **maw ha mowes**

Once you have learned the above forms it is possible to move on to asking and answering other types of questions in Cornish.

Pyth

Pyth yw ev?	What is he?	**Den yw ev.**
Pyth yns i?	What are they?	**Maw ha mowes yns i.**
Pyth yw homma?	What is this?	**Pellwolok yw homma.**

Piw

Piw yw hi?	Who is she?	**Tamsyn yw hi.**
Piw os ta?	Who are you?	**Wella ov vy.**
Piw owgh whi?	Who are you?	**Wella ha Tamsyn on ni.**

First a word about how to make plurals in Cornish. The most common way to form the plural of objects is to add -**ow** to the end of the word. For example **fordh** 'road', **fordhow** 'roads'. The most common way to make the plural of words describing a person is to add -**yon** to the word. For example **Kernow** 'Cornishman', **Kernowyon** 'Cornishmen'. There are other rules for making plurals in Cornish which will be learned at a later stage.

Some examples of using **pyth** and **piw** are given below.

Pyth yw hemma?

**Bara yw,
hemm yw bara.**

Pyth yw hemma?

**Keus yw,
hemm yw keus.**

Pyth yns i?

Pyscadoryon yns i.

Pyth yw hi?

Dyscadores yw hi.

Piw yw ev?

Mester Peber yw ev.

Piw yns i?

Mester ha
Mestres Tiek
yns i.

Practis Pymp
Exercise Five

Pyth yw ev?

Pyth yw hi?

Pyth yns i?

Pyth yns i?

Piw os ta?

Piw owgh whi?

Pyth yw hemma?

Pyth yw homma?

Dyscas Peswar
Lesson Four

Counting up to ten, objects are singular after numbers. Note that in Cornish we say: **an onen-ma yw gwynn** 'this one is white', for example, but we say **unn maw** 'one boy' and **unn venyn** 'one woman'. Note also that when **an** 'the' is used with the number 'two', it causes the Second State mutation: **an + dew/diw = an dhew, an dhiw**. Numbers 2, 3, and 4 have both masculine and feminine forms.

unn aval

dew linenner

diw *b*luven

tri loder

teyr garr

peswar morthol

peder cath

pymp defendyer

whegh scubel

seyth pluven blomm

eth hesken

naw gwelsow byhan

deg pal

In addition to the cardinal numbers (one, two, three, etc.) we have the ordinal numbers (first, second, third, etc.):

Cardinal numerals		Ordinal numerals	
1	onen	1ª	kensa
2	dew, diw	2nd, 2ª	second, nessa
3	tri, teyr	3ª	tressa
4	peswar, peder	4ª	peswora
5	pymp	5es	pympes
6	whegh	6ves	wheghves
7	seyth	7ves	seythves
8	eth	8ves	ethves
9	naw	9ves	nawves
10	deg	10ves	degves

Note that the number is put before a noun, for example: **an kensa den y'n fordh** 'the first man in the road'.

Practis Whegh
Exercise Six

Read aloud the following and translate into English:

Dedh da, piw os ta? Wella ov vy, ha piw os ta jy? Tamsyn ov vy. Drog yw an gewer hedhyw. Yw, mes nyns yw yeyn. Fatla genes, Tamsyn? O, da lowr ov vy, mes cales yw an ober scol. Pyth yw ober an scol? Dew bractis yw gans linenner ha pluven blomm. Nyns yw henna cales, Tamsyn. Yw, mes dedh frank a vydh an jedh avorow, ha my a vydh lowen avorow y'n park gans peder cowethes ha deg fardellik cresigow. My o lowen de y'n cinema. Da o an second fylm. Fylm adro dhe wragh o.

New words: **adro** 'about, concerning', **cales** 'hard, difficult', **coweth** 'male friend', **cowethes (an gowethes)** 'female friend', **cresigow** 'crisps', **da** 'good', **fardellik** 'packet', **frank** 'free', **fylm** 'film', **gans** 'with', **cinema** 'cinema', **jy** suffixed form of 'you' used for emphasis, **o** 'oh', **ober** 'work', **park** 'park, field', **scol (scol vras)** 'school'.

Dyscas Pymp
Lesson Five

In this lesson we learn about other verbs. Remember that a verb is a word that describes an action. First we need to know about verbal particles or prefixes to the verbs. We have already learned how to say "no" using the verbal particle for 'not'—we place **na** or **nag** before the verb (**na** becomes **nag** before **a, e, eu, i, o, u,** and **y,** if the intial vowel begins any part of the verb **bos** 'be' or **mos** 'go').

To say that something is not, we use the negative particle **ny** or **nyns** (before **a, e, eu, i, o, u,** and **y**) before the verb.

To make a statement we place **y** or **yth** (before **a, e, eu, i, o, u,** and **y**) before the verb.

These three particles cause mutations. In Lesson One we learned about *Second State* mutation. The particles **na/nag, ny/nyns,** and **a** all cause Second State mutation of any verb that follows.

The particle **a** is a bit complicated. At the beginning of a sentence, before the verb, **a** indicates that a question is being asked. When it comes after the subject of the sentence, or after the verb, **a** is a verbal particle.

To link the verb 'to be' with a following verb to make a present-tense statement we place **ow** or **owth** (before **a, e, eu, i, o, u,** and **y**) before the verb. The particle **ow** causes the *Fourth State* mutation which we will learn more about in Lesson Six. In this lesson we will use examples that don't show this mutation, in order to keep things simple.

The "long forms" of the verb **bos** 'to be' are given in the next page. These forms come at the beginning of the sentence, and can be followed by **ow** + the verb to make a simple present-tense sentence.

Yth esov vy **ow redya**	I am reading
Yth esos ta **ow revya**	You are rowing
Yma ev **ow cosca**	He is sleeping
Yma hi **ow neyja**	She is swimming
Yth eson ni **owth eva**	We are drinking
Yth esowgh whi **ow kerdhes**	You are walking
Ymons i **ow marhogeth**	They are riding (a horse)

In Cornish, as in other languages, we also have auxiliary or helper verbs. These are:

gul 'to do', **mynnes** 'to will, to wish', **gallos** 'to be able'

The third person singular, or 'he'/'she' forms of these verbs are **gwra**, **mynn**, and **gyll**. We use these forms to give the "impersonal" forms of the verbs as below.

my a wra	**my a vynn**	**my a yll**
ty a wra	**ty a vynn**	**ty a yll**
ev a wra	**ev a vynn**	**ev a yll**
hi a wra	**hi a vynn**	**hi a yll**
ni a wra	**ni a vynn**	**ni a yll**
whi a wra	**whi a vynn**	**whi a yll**
i a wra	**i a vynn**	**i a yll**

These helper verbs can be followed by other verbs. That's why we call them helper verbs, because they help you to use other verbs in a simple way.

Examples of other verbs: **cavos** 'to have, to find, to get', **cara** 'to love, to like', **cosca** 'to sleep', **don** 'carry', **donsya** 'to dance', **dos** 'to come', **dybry** 'to eat', **eva** 'to drink', **gwary** 'to play', **gweles** ' to see', **kerdhes** 'to walk', **marhogeth** 'to ride', **mos** 'to go', **neyja** 'to fly, to swim', **ponya** 'to run', **redya** 'to read', **revya** 'to row'.

A noun subject can come before the verb, e.g. **An den a wra gweles an flogh** 'the man will see the child' or, if the subject is a noun, or if 'he' or 'she' is used, we can ask a question e.g. **A wra an den gweles**

an flogh? 'Will the man see the child?' **A yll hi redya yn ta?** 'Can she read well?' **A vynn ev mos dhe'n cinema?** 'Will he go to the cinema?'

Remember when we learned to talk about the weather we learned how to say 'yes' and 'no'? We learned that in Cornish the answer had to match the form of the verb. It is the same here: the answer to the first question above can be **Gwra** or **Na wra**, the answer to the second question can be **Gyll** or **Na yll**, the answer to the third can be **Mynn** or **Na vynn**.

We will learn to ask other types of questions in later lessons.

An important thing to observe about Cornish is that the present tense of **gul** and **mynnes** are usually used with a future meaning. So both **my a wra redya** and **my a vynn redya** mean 'I will read'. As noted above, to say I read' or 'I am reading' in good Cornish we say **yth esov vy ow redya**. To say 'I want to read' we use a special form of the verb **cara** 'to love, to like': **my a garsa redya**. This might seem a little complicated but in practice you can build sentences easily:

Yth esov vy **ow redya**	I am reading, I read
My a wra **redya**	I will read
My a vynn **redya**	I will read
My a garsa **redya**	I want to read

Practis Seyth
Exercise Seven

Read, understand and translate into English the examples below;
New words: **margh** 'horse', **mar pleg** 'please', **torth a vara** 'loaf of bread'.

Ev a wra don an trog dillas.

. . . .

My a garsa cavos dehen rew, a vamm.

. . . .

An ki a vynn dybry an ascorn.

. . . .

Whi a yll cosca y'n tylda-na.

. . . .

Hi a wra gwary gans pel.

. . . .

Brav yw an gewer;
ni a yll neyja y'n mor.

. . . .

An vowes a vynn marhogeth
war an margh-na.

. . . .

My a garsa cavos torth a vara mar pleg.

. . . .

New words: **dhe** 'to', **lyver** 'book', **treth** 'beach', **war** 'on'.

Ty a yll gwary war an treth.

. . . .

I a wra revya an scath.

. . . .

Ev a garsa mos dhe Loundres.

. . . .

Hi a vynn ponya dhe scol.

. . . .

Answer the following questions:

A yll ev redya lyver?

. . . .

A yll hi don an gyst boos-ma?

. . . .

A wra an maw dos gans coweth?

. . . .

A yll an ki gweles an gath?

. . . .

Dyscas Whegh
Lesson Six

In this lesson we revise and add to some of the points that we have already learned.

Here are some more greetings:

Myttin da!*	Good morning!
Dohajedh da!	Good afternoon!
Gorthuher da!	Good evening!
Nos da!	Good night!
Gromercy!	Thanks!
Meur ras!	Thanks!

A reminder that English and Cornish are often quite different is often helpful. Learners often try to use an English structure to say something not knowing that Cornish says it in a different way. For example, ***Glawek yw hi hedhyw** is wrong. This means "she is rainy today". The right way to say "It is raining today" is **Glaw a wra hedhyw**, or **Yma ow cul glaw hedhyw**. Similarly, instead of ***Erhek yw hi hedhyw**, the impersonal **Ergh a wra hedhyw** or **Yma ow cul ergh hedhyw** should be used.

---

* The 'i' of **myttin** is pronounced like the 'y' and is so spelt in historical Cornish, that is, *myttyn*.

Practis Eth
Exercise Eight

Kescows yn Popty
Conversation in a Bakery

Read aloud and then take parts and perform the playlet.

Mestres Tiek Myttin da.

Peber Myttin da, Mestres Tiek, fatla genowgh whi?

Mestres Tiek Ogh, da lowr ov vy. Fatel vydh an gewer hedhyw?

Peber Y whra glaw *kyns* nos, yth esov ow *tyby*.

Mestres Tiek Mes tomm yw an gewer *lemmyn*. My a vynn cavos hedhyw diw dorth a vara ha whegh *tesen vyhan* ha *tesen safron*.

Peber Diw dorth a vara, whegh tesen vyhan, ha tesen safron. Yw henna oll?

Mestres Tiek Yw.

Peber Henn yw eth *peuns poran*.

Mestres Tiek My a vynn gorra an bara y'n sagh-ma ha'n desen y'n *sagh*-na.

Peber Honn yw fordh da. Duw genowgh whi.

Mestres Tiek Duw genowgh whi!

New words: **kyns** 'before', **lemmyn** 'now', **peuns** 'pound sterling', **poran** 'exactly', **sagh** 'bag', **tesen vyhan** 'bun', **tesen safron** 'saffron cake', **tyby** 'to suppose'.

Why not try to write your own story about a meeting in a shop?

Here is a table of the Second State and Fourth State mutations:

First	Second	Fourth
p-	b-	—
b-	v-	p-
m-	v-	—
f-	(v-)	—
t-	d-	—
d-	dh-	t-
ch-	j-	—
s-	(z-)	—
ke-	ge-	—
ki-	gi-	—
ky-	gy-	—
ca-	ga-	—
co-	go-	—
cu-	gu-	—
qw-	gw-	—
cl-	gl-	—
cr-	gr-	—
kn-	gn-	—
ge-	e-	ke-
gi-	i-	ki-
gy-	y-	ky-
ga-	a-	ca-
go-	wo-	co-
gu-	wu-	cu-
gw-	w-	qw-
gl-	l-	cl-
gn-	n-	—
gre-	re-	cre-
gri-	ri-	cri-
gry-	ry-	cry-
gra-	ra-	cra-
gro-	wro-	cro-
gru-	wru-	cru-

Other letters have no mutation.

About the Fourth State Mutation

The Fourth State mutation affects the letters **b**, **d**, **g** and **gw**. A good way to remember Fourth State mutation is to think of it as a "backwards" mutation from the Second State. So **b** changes to **p**, **d** changes to **t**, **g** changes to **c** or **k** (depending on the vowel that follows) and **gw** changes to **qw**. Remember that **ow** becomes **owth** before a vowel.

Examples of the particle **ow** used with the verbal noun to form the present participle (also called the "verbal adjective"): **ow pewa** 'living' (from **bewa** 'to live'), **ow tybry** 'eating' (from **dybry** 'to eat'), **ow qwandra** 'wandering' (from **gwandra** 'to wander'). It occurs after **mar** or **mara** 'if': **mar callav** 'if I am able', **mara qwrav vy** 'if I do it'. Note that in verbs of **bos** and **mos** the form is **mars**: **mars usy yn Kernow** 'if he is in Cornwall', **Mars av vy lemmyn** 'if I go now'.

About the Second State Mutation

After the definite article **an** when the noun is feminine singular, e.g. **an venyn** 'the woman', or when it is a masculine plural of people, e.g. **an byscadoryon** 'the fishermen', except where the noun is a late borrowing from English or other languages, like **an doctours** 'the doctors'. The masculine nouns **an vergh** 'the horses' and **an varchons** 'the merchants' are exceptional. **An** also mutates the word **tra** 'thing': **an dra** 'the thing'.

The adjective is mutated after a feminine noun in the singular or after a masculine noun referring to people in the plural: **benyn dha** 'a good women', **pyscadoryon lyb** 'wet fishermen' (from **glyb**).

Second State mutation occurs after **unn** 'one' when the following noun is feminine singular: **unn venyn** 'one woman'. **Unn** also mutates **tra** 'thing': **unn dra** 'one thing'.

Second State mutation occurs after **dew** and **diw** 'two: **dew dhen** 'two men', **diw venyn** 'two women'. Also the initial letter of **dew/diw** is mutated by **an** 'the': **an dhiw gath** 'the two cats'. **Dhe** 'to' also causes mutation to a following word. Don't forget also that the verbal particle **a** causes mutation, as in **my a wra** 'I will do, I will make', as well as the question particle **a** and the negative particles **ny** and **na**.

Other causes of Second State mutation will be covered in later lessons or more advanced studies.

Kernewek adro dhyn
Cornish around us

eglos		**pons**	
bre (an vre)		**logh**	
carn		**penntir**	

Rann Dew
Part Two

At the end of part two of this book you should be able to:

- Understand a range of familiar spoken phrases
- Understand and read out familiar written phrases
- Answer simple questions and give basic information
- Write one or two short sentences to a model and fill in words on a simple form

Dyscas Seyth
Lesson Seven

In Lesson Three of this book we learned about the verb, **bos** 'to be'. What we learned was the "short form" of this verb which is used to describe what something is like. In Lesson Five we had a brief peek at the "long form" of **bos**. We'll now learn more about the "long form" which is used to describe the position of something or a continuous action.

First of all, we need to know some words that describe position in Cornish:

adrev 'behind, **dherag** 'in front of', **ryb** 'beside', **war** 'on', **yn dann** 'under', **yn** 'in', **y'n** 'in the'. The words **war** and **yn dann** cause *Second State* mutation

Below the long form of **bos** is given in the present tense in sample statements. Note that the particle **yth** is used because a vowel follows.

Yth esov vy **ryb an margh.**

Yth eson ni **adrev an fos.**
(pronounced **adrev an vos**)

Yth esos ta yn dann an lawlen.

Yth esowgh whi dherag an imach.

Yma ev dherag an carr.

Ymons i yn Loundres.

Yma hi war an lesk lovan.

As well as persons of the verb we can describe the position of other things. For example: **yma'n gath yn dann an gwely** 'the cat is under the bed'.

In order to ask questions in the long form of **bos** we leave off the particle, and in the third person the forms are **usy** and **esons**:

Esov vy ryb an margh?
Esos ta yn dann an lawlen?
Usy ev dherag an carr?
Usy hi war an lesk lovan?

Eson ni adrev an fos?
Esowgh whi dherag an imach?
Esons i yn Loundres?

To reply 'yes' to a question we repeat the verb, as shown above, in the correct person: **Esons, ymons i yn Loundres** 'Yes, they are in London'. To reply 'no' to a question we place **nag** before the question forms. To say something 'is not' we place **nyns** before the question forms. The pattern is easy to remember: **Nag esons, nyns esons i yn scol** 'No, they are not in school'. Here are examples of the negative answers in each of the persons of the verb.

Nag esov, nyns esov vy **ryb an margh.**
Nag esos, nyns esos ta **yn dann an lawlen.**
Nag usy, nyns usy ev **dherag an carr.**
Nag usy, nyns usy hi **war an lesk lovan.**
Nag eson, nyns eson ni **adrev an fos.**
Nag esowgh, nyns esowgh whi **dherag an imach.**
Nag esons, nyns esons i **yn Loundres.**

Note that in the 'no' answer forms there is no suffixed pronoun. Note also that there is a special question form which is used when the subject is indefinite:

Eus den dherag an chi? 'Is there a man in front of the house?
Eus, yma den dherag an chi. 'Yes, there is a man in front of the house.'

Practis Naw
Exercise Nine

This exercise starts with some sample questions and answers. Complete the answers for the following questions. *New words*: **astel** 'board', **mordardh** 'surf'.

Usy ev y'n gwely?
Usy, yma ev y'n gwely.

Esos ta war an lesk lovan?
Nag esov, yth esov vy war astel omborth.

Eus cath y'n lowarth?
Nag eus, yma ki y'n lowarth.

Esov vy yn dann an lawlen?
Nag esos, yth esos yn dann an glaw!

Esons i dherag an jynn tenna?

Esov vy adrev an garrek?

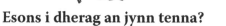

Eson ni yn Brystow?

Usy an den yn dann an garrek?

Eus corev y'n wedren?

Esos ta ryb an gyst?

Usy an gador ryb an fos?

Usy an vowes war astel mordardh?

When you have finished this, as a group or class exercise, place objects in different positions in relation to one another and ask each other questions. such as: **Usy an bluven war an gador?** 'Is the pen on the chair'. Then reply: **usy** 'yes' or **nag usy** 'no'. This can be followed by a statement about where the object actually is, such as **Yma'n bluven war an lyver.**

Notes on possessives

In Cornish if we wish to say 'the tail of the dog' we say **lost an ki**, literally 'tail the dog'. You may have seen houses named **Gwel an Mor** this means 'a view of the sea'. Note also that we signify possession in Cornish by placing the object possessed before the the name of the owner e.g. **pel Peder** 'Peter's ball'. As we know **dhe** means 'to', **dhe** is also used to show ownership, as in **yma pel dhe Beder** 'Peter owns a ball'.

Practis Deg • *Exercise Ten*
Redyans • *Reading*

Read the following passage and translate, if you're stuck look at the picture on the next page:

Yth esov vy yn chi Wella ha Tamsyn. Esowgh whi omma, Wella ha Tamsyn? Eson, yth eson ni y'n stevel esedha. Y'n stevel esedha yma strel war an leur ha flourys war an bellwolok. Ynwedh, yma liwans war an fos. Yma ki dhe Wella ha Tamsyn. Usy an ki omma? Usy, yma ev ryb an gador hir. Pyth yw hanow an ki? Hanow an ki yw Lostek. Eus cath dhe Wella ha Tamsyn? Eus, yma cath yn dann an voos. Yma an gath ow cosca ena. Yma lyver war an voos ha Tamsyn a vynn redya an lyver. Wella yw trist, ny yll ev mos yn mes hedhyw, glyb yw an gewer. Wella a garsa gwary pel droos.

New words: **cador hir** 'sofa', **ena** 'there', **leur** 'floor', **liwans** 'painting', **moos, an voos** 'table, the table', **omma** 'here', **pel droos** 'football', **stevel esedha** 'sitting room', **strel** 'mat, rug', **yn mes** 'outside', **ynwedh** 'also'.

Is there anything else in this picture that you could talk about using what you have learned so far?

Dyscas Eth
Lesson Eight

In this lesson we learn about the other use of the long form of the verb **bos** 'to be'. In English if we want to describe an action that continues over a period of time we place '-ing' after the verb, as in *walking, running, singing,* and so on. In Cornish we place the particle **ow** in front of the verbal noun. **Ow** causes the Fourth State mutation.

Practis Unnek
Exercise Eleven

Referring to the table of mutations on page 28, write the verbs in the following expressions as they appear before Fourth State mutation is applied. So for **ow tybry** the answer is **dybry**.

ow pewa 'living'   **ow talleth** 'beginning'

.... 'to live'   .... 'to begin'

ow corra 'putting'   **ow qweles** 'seeing'

.... 'to put'   .... 'to see'

ow tonsya 'dancing'   **ow ponkya** 'knocking, hitting'

.... 'to dance'   .... 'to knock, to hit'

ow colya 'sailing'   **ow qwary** 'playing'

.... 'to sail'   .... 'to play'

Practis Dewdhek
Exercise Twelve

To follow are some pictures of actions and a phrase underneath. Use the pictures to work out the meaning of the phrase in English. The first two have been done for you.

Yma ev ow scrifa.
'He is writing.'

Yth esov vy owth eva.
'I am drinking.'

Yth eson ni ow qwevya.

....

Ymons i ow neyja.

....

Yma hi ow lemmel.

....

Yth esowgh whi owth esedha.

....

Yth esos ta ow redya.   **Yma ev ow potya.**

....

Yma hi ow marhogeth   **Ymons i ow wherthin.**
war dhiwros.

....

We saw in Lesson Seven that it is possible to ask questions and make
positive or negative answers using the long form of **bos**. Of course
questions and answers both positive and negative can also be
expressed with the long form of **bos** (**esov**, **esos**, etc.) when followed
by the participle form, i.e. **ow**[4] + verbal noun of other verbs. Examples:

Usy ev ow cana? 'Is he singing?'
Usy, yma ev ow cana 'Yes, he is singing'

Esons ow tonsya? 'Are they dancing?'
Nag esons, ymons i ow lemmel 'No, they are jumping'.

With any verb in Cornish we can also ask a negative question by
placing the question particle **a** before the verb. Examples:

A nyns usy ev ow cana? 'Isn't he singing?'
A ny vydh an gewer brav hedhyw? 'Won't the weather be fine today?'

Dyscas Naw
Lesson Nine

In Lesson Four, we learned how to count up to ten in Cornish. As we are about to learn how to tell the time in Cornish, we need to know how to count up to 29. First of all we'll learn the numbers 11 to 20, and some new words. Remember, in Cornish we do not use plurals after numbers.

unnek edhen

dewdhek hanaf

tredhek collel

peswardhek ros

**pymthek
tykky Duw**

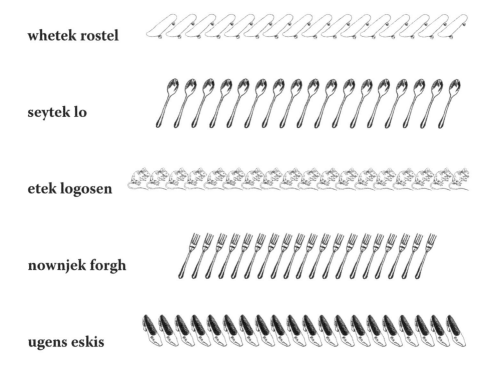

whetek rostel

seytek lo

etek logosen

nownjek forgh

ugens eskis

To count beyond 20 up to 39 we refer to the number being 'on the' twenty: **unnek warn ugens** 'thirty-one' ('11 on the 20'), **naw warn ugens** 'twenty-nine'. Note that **warn** is a special form of **war an** 'on the', used only in counting.

Telling the Time

In order to tell the time in Cornish, there are some additional words to learn. There are two words which mean 'hour' in Cornish. First there is the word **our**, which we use if we are talking about a number of hours: **my a wra dos yn peswar our** 'I shall come in four hours' time'. An 'hour o'clock' in Cornish is **eur**, and this is a feminine noun. So we say for example **diw eur** 'two o'clock', **teyr eur** 'three o'clock' **peder eur** 'four o'clock', using the feminine forms of the numbers two, three and four.

We have learned the word **dhe** meaning 'to'; this is used to signify 'before the hour', as in **pymp mynysen dhe deyr eur** 'five minutes to three'. Another new word, **wosa** or **woja**, meaning 'after' is needed to signify 'after the hour', as in **pymp mynysen wosa teyr eur** 'five minutes after three'.

All we need now is the word for 'quarter', **qwartron**, and the word for 'half', **hanter**. Note the use of **hanter** in these words: **hanter dedh** 'noon, midday', and **hanter nos** 'midnight'. And finally... to ask the time we say **py eur yw?**

Practis Tredhek
Exercise Thirteen

Below are a number of clock faces telling different times, write under each one the time in Cornish. **Py eur yw?**

....

....

....

....

....

....

45

Other Plural Forms

In Lesson Three of this book we learned how to make plurals in Cornish by adding **-ow** to some words and **-yon** to make a plural of persons. Other words have the vowels changed in other ways to make the plural.

davas 'a sheep'	**deves** 'some sheep'
men 'a stone'	**meyn** 'stones'.

Other words, especially (but not only) words referring to animals, have **-es** added:

cath 'cat'	**cathes** 'cats'
bugh 'cow'	**buhes** 'cows'
flogh 'child'	**flehes** 'children'.

Words which have been historically borrowed into Cornish from English tend to make plurals with **-s** or **-ys**:

rom 'room'	**romys** 'rooms'
cothman 'friend'	**cothmans** 'friends'.

Plant names especially drop an **-en** singular ending to form a collective plural:

gwedhen 'tree'	**gwydh** '(lots of) trees'
banallen 'broom bush'	**banal** '(lots of) broom'.

With regard to parts of the body, we speak in Cornish of having two of these:

lagas 'eye'	**dewlagas** 'eyes'
garr 'leg'	**diwar** 'legs', 'shanks'.

Practis Peswardhek
Exercise Fourteen

Below is a passage of Cornish, read it aloud and make sure you understand most of it. After this answer the questions following the passage writing your answers in Cornish.

Eth eur yw hag yma Wella ha *tas* ow tybry *hansel*. Tas a wra *leverel* dhe Wella: Ni a wra *mos* dhe'n park hedhyw. Naw eur yw hag ymons i ow mos dhe'n park. Y'n park yma lesk lovan. Yma Wella ow cara marhogeth war an lesk lovan. Yma Wella war an lesk lovan hag yma tas adrev an lesk lovan. Tas a vynn *herdhya* Wella. Wella yw lowen. Wosa an lesk lovan Wella a vynn marhogeth war astel omborth. Mes tas yw *re* boos rag esedha war an astel omborth. Yma cothman Wella y'n park, pyth yw hanow cothman Wella? Peder yw. A vynn Peder marhogeth gans Wella? Mynn. Ymons i war an astel omborth.

Hanter wosa deg eur yw hag yma Wella ha tas ow mos dhe'n *bosty*. Wella a vynn cavos dehen rew. Ny vynn tas cavos dehen rew, ev a vynn *prena* hanaf *coffy*. Tas a wra leverel, "My a garsa cavos dehen rew ha hanaf coffy." Qwartron wosa unnek eur yw; i a wra mos *tre*.

New words: **bosty** 'café', **coffy** 'coffee', **tre** 'home(wards)', **erhy** 'to order', **hansel** 'breakfast', **herdhya** 'to push', **leverel** 'to say', **mos** 'to go', **prena** 'to buy', **re** 'too' (causes Second State mutation), **tas** 'father'.

What time do Wella and his dad take breakfast?

....

What does Wella's dad tell him?

....

What time do they go to the park?

....

What will Wella's dad do for him in the park?

....

What is the name of Wella's friend?

....

Why can't Wella's dad go on the see-saw?

....

What time do they go to the café?

....

What does Wella's dad order in the café?

....

Dyscas Deg
Lesson Ten

Personal Forms of the Auxiliary Verbs

We have learned the impersonal forms of these verbs. These are fine if you only wish to make statements. In order to ask and answer questions or make negative statements, however, it is necessary to know the personal forms of these verbs. Below these verbs are listed without particles or suffixed pronouns. It is good practice to recite these a number of times column by column so that you get used to saying them.

	To do	To wish or want	To be able
I	**gwrav, gwrama**	**mynnav**	**gallav**
Thou	**gwredh, gwreta**	**mynnydh, mynta**	**gyllydh, gylta**
He/she	**gwra**	**mynn**	**gyll**
We	**gwren**	**mynnyn**	**gyllyn**
You	**gwrewgh**	**mynnowgh**	**gyllowgh**
They	**gwrons**	**mynnons**	**gyllons**

To make statements from these forms it is necessary to place the particle **y** before the verb. The particle **y** causes mutation of the following letter to the Fifth State. Don't worry too much about this at this stage. You just need to remember how this effects the auxiliary verbs; **gw** becomes **wh**, **m** becomes **f**, and **g** becomes **h**. Examples: **y whrav**, **y fynn**, and **y hyllyn**. We will remember that the question particle **a**, the negative particle **na**, and the negative answer particle **ny** all cause Second State mutation. We can use the question words **pyth** 'what' and **fatel** 'how' with these verbs.

We have learned that in Cornish it is particularly important that for questions and answers the correct form of the verb must be used. For example, to the question "**A vynnydh cavos dehen rew?**" the answer "**Mynn**" is *wrong*; the correct answer is "**Mynnav**".

New words: **dhe ves** 'away', **di** 'as far as that', **degolyow hav** 'a summer holiday', **heb dout** 'without doubt', **kemeres** 'to take', **mar** 'if' (**mars** before vowels), **mires orth** 'look at', **na fors** 'never mind', **ostel** 'hotel', **ostya** 'to lodge', **pub** 'every', **rag** 'for the purpose of', **skeusennow** 'photographs', **tren** 'train', **universita** 'university', **vysytya** 'visit'.

Kembra

castel, pl. castylly

hens'horn an als

Practis Pymthek
Exercise Fifteen

The following is a conversation between Wella and Tamsyn about a forthcoming holiday. Read it and understand it. After this take the parts of Wella and Tamsyn and perform it as a short play putting suitable expression into the phrases.

Wella   Ytho Tamsyn, a vynnowgh whi mos dhe ves rag an degolyow hav?

Tamsyn   Heb dout, ni a wra mos dhe Gembra.

Wella   Fatel wrewgh whi mos di?

Tamsyn   Ni a wra mos ena yn carr.

Wella   Pyth a vynnowgh whi gul yn Kembra?

Tamsyn   My a vynn mos dhe'n treth mes heb dout Mamm ha Tas a vynn mires orth castylly.

Wella   A yllydh neyja, Tamsyn?

Tamsyn   Gallav, my a yll neyja yn ta.

Wella   Ny allav neyja yn ta mes y hallav marhogeth astel mordardh, *pur* dha ov vy.

Tamsyn   Y whren ni ostya yn ostel ryb an mor yn Aberystwyth. Y hallav neyja pub dedh mar pydh da an gewer. Tre vras yw Aberystwyth hag yma universita ena. Ynwedh yma hens'horn an als ena ha tren byhan.

Wella   A wrewgh whi mos war hens'horn an als?

Tamsyn   Y fynnav mos, mes an problem yw Mamm ha Tas. Y fynnons i vysytya castylly.

Wella   Na fors, da yw mires orth castylly ynwedh. Yma *lies* castel bras yn Kembra. A vynta kemeres skeusennow?

Tamsyn   Na vynnav, mes Tas a vynn.

Wella   A vynnav vy gweles skeusennow degolyow an hav?

Tamsyn   Mynnydh, heb dout.

Notes: The word **pur** is an intensifier and means 'very', it causes Second State mutation: **pur** + **da** = **pur dha** 'very good', **pur** + **coth** = **pur goth** 'very old', **pur** + **glyb** = **pur lyb** 'very wet'. The word **lies** means 'many' and is followed by the noun in the singular form: **yma lies pysk omma** 'there are many fish here', 'there are lots of fish here'.

Dyscas Unnek
Lesson Eleven

Prepositional pronouns

A complicated name and perhaps a complicated idea for a native English speaker. We have already learned the words **gans** 'with', and **dhe** 'to'; in Cornish instead of just saying 'with us', 'to him', etc., there are personal forms to learn just as we have learned personal forms for the verbs.

	Gans		*Dhe*
with me	**genev**	to me	**dhymm, dhymmo**
with thee	**genes**	to thee	**dhis, dhiso**
with him	**ganso**	to him	**dhodho**
with her	**gensy**	to her	**dhedhy**
with us	**genen**	to us	**dhyn**
with you	**genowgh**	to you	**dhywgh**
with them	**gansa**	to them	**dhedha**

In Cornish **dhe** 'to', is used to show ownership, as in **yma astel mordardh dhodho** 'he owns a surf board'. Suffixed pronouns may be added to any of the above. When this is done the statement is more emphatic. Compare **Yma pellwolok loren dhedha i** 'They've got satellite TV!' and **Yma pellwolok loren dhedha** 'They have a satellite television'.

Practis Whetek
Exercise Sixteen

Read the following statements aloud and then translate them into good English (not direct literal translations). For **gans** you can sometimes translate to 'I have got', 'Have you got' etc.

Eus pluven genes? ....

Yma ki dhodho. ....

Yma an tanbrennyer gansa i. ....

Yma gwreg dhymm. ....

Yma'n ki ganso. ....

Eus cares dhiso? ....

Y fydh Wella genen haneth. ....

Yth esa ki dhyn. ....

Yth esa Peder gensy nyhewer. ....

Yma ev ow cowsel orthowgh. ....

New words: **cares** 'girlfriend', **cowsel** 'to speak', **esa** 'he/she was' (*past of* **yma**), **haneth** 'this evening, tonight', **nyhewer** 'last night', **orthowgh** 'at you, to you' (**cowsel** takes the preposition **orth**; see page 74 below), **sugra** 'sugar', **tanbrennyer** 'matches', **te** 'tea'.

*Idiomatic use of **gans** and **dhe***

There are a number of equivalents of expressions in English which are said in Cornish using prepositions in **gans** and **dhe**. For example: **drog yw genev** 'I am sorry', **da yw genev** 'I am pleased', 'I like', and **gwell yw genev** 'I prefer', but **gwell yw dhymm** 'I had better', also **res yw dhymm** 'I must'. Translate the following expressions into English:

Y fydh Wella genen haneth. ....

Drog yw genen, nyns eus sugra. ....

Gwell yw genev te. ....

Res o dhodho cavos bara. ....

Da yw gensy cosca yn tylda. ....

Gwell yw dhywgh mos tre. ....

Da vydh gensy neyja y'n mor. ....

Now would be a good time to review the Fourth State mutation. Turn back to page 28 and review the table and the summary of causes of the mutation.

Rann Tri
Part Three

At the end of part three of this book you should be able to:

- Understand the main points from a short spoken passage made up of familiar language
- Understand the main points from a short written text in clear printed script
- Ask and answer simple questions and talk about your interests
- Write a few short sentences with support, using expressions which you have already learned

Dyscas Dewdhek
Lesson Twelve

In this lesson we learn how to express possession in Cornish. We use the possessive pronouns which are:

ow³	dha²	y²	hy³	agan	agas	aga³
my	thy	his	her	our	your	their

You will note that **dha²** and **y²** require mutation of a following letter to the Second State and **ow³**, **hy³**, and **aga³** require mutation of a following letter to a new Third State mutation. Here are some examples using these latter forms which indicate which letters are affected and how.

ow *h*anstel
(< **canstel**)

ow *f*luven
(< **pluven**)

hy *f*adel
(< **padel**)

aga *th*avern
(< **tavern**)

hi *th*roos
(< **troos**)

aga *wh*eth
(< **qweth**)

ow *h*offy
(< **coffy**)

ow *th*anses
(< **tanses**)

Rannow an Corf

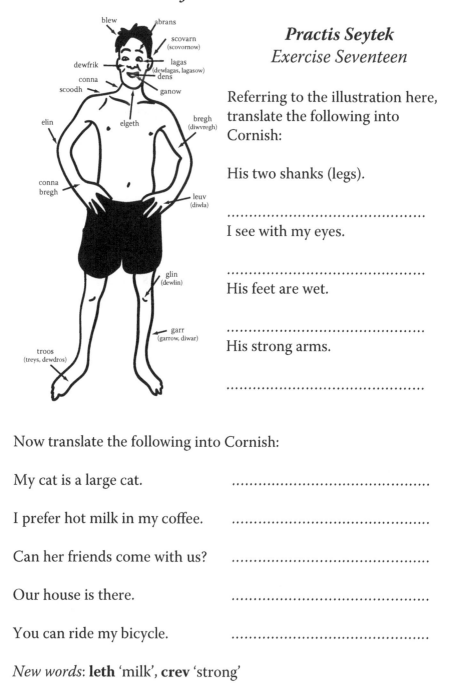

blew
abrans
scovarn
(scovornow)
dewfrik
lagas
(dewlagas, lagasow)
conna
dens
scoodh
ganow
elin
elgeth
bregh
(diwvregh)
conna
bregh
leuv
(diwla)
glin
(dewlin)
garr
(garrow, diwar)
troos
(treys, dewdros)

Practis Seytek
Exercise Seventeen

Referring to the illustration here, translate the following into Cornish:

His two shanks (legs).

....

I see with my eyes.

....

His feet are wet.

....

His strong arms.

....

Now translate the following into Cornish:

My cat is a large cat. ....

I prefer hot milk in my coffee. ....

Can her friends come with us? ....

Our house is there. ....

You can ride my bicycle. ....

New words: **leth** 'milk', **crev** 'strong'

Dyscas Tredhek
Lesson Thirteen

The possessive pronouns are used in another important way in Cornish. Whereas in English we would say 'I'll see you', in Cornish we must say the equivalent of (literally) 'I will your seeing', which is: **My a vynn agas gweles**. Also possessive pronouns can be used in this way to talk about objects as well as people.

Practis Etek
Exercise Eighteen

Below are some statements in Cornish which use this form. Translate them into English, you may have to unmutate some verbs in order to recognize them.

Gwell yw genev y weles avorow.

....

Ny allav vy aga havos.

....

Res yw dhodho y redya y'n scol.

....

My a yll hy gweles war an vre.

....

Peder, ny allav vy dha dhon, poos os ta.

....

A vynta ow revya dres an dowr?

....

Ny vynnons i agan clowes.

....

Ny a yll agas metya ryb clock an dre.

....

New words: **dres** 'over', **dowr** 'water, river', **clowes** 'to hear', **metya** 'to meet', **clock** 'clock'.

You will often hear Cornish speakers saying **dha weles** or **agas gweles** as a form of goodbye. This of course is a shortening of the full statements **y fynnav dha weles** and **y fynnav agas gweles**.

There are some additional words that you need to know to expand conversation. These are: **pub** 'each, every', **keniver** 'every, so many', **nepprys** 'sometime', (with negative) 'anytime', **pub prys** 'all the time'.

We can now make statements like:

My a vynn dha weles nepprys.
   'I'll see you sometime.'

Ymons i ow cowsel Kernowek pub prys.
   'They speak Cornish all the time.'

Usy ev ow cowsel Kernowek keniver dedh?
   'Does he speak Cornish every day?'

You should now be able to make your conversation less stilted and more lively. Try out things with your fellow students.

Dyscas Peswardhek
Lesson Fourteen

*Past Tense (Preterite) of the auxiliary verb **gul** and the Past
(Imperfect) of the auxiliary verbs **mynnes** and **gallos***

We have learned the personal forms of **gul** 'do', **mynnes** 'will', and
gallos 'can, be able' in the present tense. In order to widen our
conversation we are now about to learn the past tense (preterite) of
gul and the past (imperfect) of **mynnes** and **gallos**. The paradigms
are cited in full below without particles in front of them. Again
practise saying each of these a number of times so that you get used
to the pronunciation.

	To do	To wish or want	To be able
I	**gwrug**	**mynnen**	**gyllyn**
Thou	**gwrussys, gwrusta**	**mynnes**	**gyllys**
He/she	**gwrug**	**mynna**	**gylly**
We	**gwrussyn**	**mynnen**	**gyllyn**
You	**gwrussowgh**	**mynnewgh**	**gyllewgh**
They	**gwrussons**	**mynnens**	**gyllens**

Practis Nawnjek • *Exercise Nineteen*

Here is a passage making use of some of the above forms. Read it and
answer the questions in Cornish that follow it.

Dedh da, Morwena. A wrusta mos dhe'n dre hedhyw? Gwrug, my a vynna *prenassa*. Fatel o an *dro*? O, da lowr. My a wrug gweles flehes Angove. *Pandr'*esens i ow cul y'n dre? Yth esens i ow mos dhe'n cinema. Res o dhymm mos dhe'n kiger rag prena *kig on* ha *selsik*. A ny wrusta gonis yn *gwerthjy* kiger? Gwrug, mes ny yllyn vy *pesya* y'n tyller wosa an flehes. My a vynna prena *fav ledan* hedhyw, mes an gwerthjy a wrug aga *gwertha* oll. *Ytho*, me a wrug prena *pys*, *patatys*, ha *cowl*. Wosa prenassa my a wrug mos dhe'n *vedhegva* saw ny ylly an *kyttrin* mos an *fordh*-na. O res dhis gweles an *medhek*? Nyns o res dhymm y weles, mes my a vynna cavos ow *medhegneth*. Prag na yllys dos genev vy dhe'n vedhegva y'm carr de? Ny yllyn dos genes, rag yth esa whans dhymm mos dhe weles ow mamm de. *Ogh soweth*, well, *ny vern*. Da o genev dha weles, Morwena.

New words: **esens** 'they were' (past tense of **esons**), **fav ledan** 'broad beans', **fordh** 'way, road', **gwertha** 'to sell', **gwerthjy** 'shop', **kig on** 'lamb (meat)', **kyttrin** 'bus' (or use **buss**), **medhegneth** 'medicine', **medhegva** 'surgery', **medhek** '(medical) doctor', **ny vern** 'never mind', **ogh soweth** 'oh what a pity', **pandra** 'what' (literally 'what thing', used before verbs, causes omission of particle and Second State mutation), **pesya** 'to continue', **prenassa** 'to shop', **pys** 'peas', **tro (an dro)** 'a turn, a stroll', **tyller** 'place', **ytho** 'then, so'.

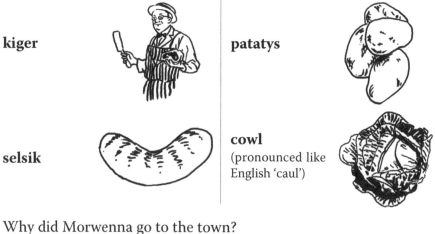

kiger

patatys

selsik

cowl
(pronounced like English 'caul')

Why did Morwenna go to the town?

....

Whom did she see there?

....

What did they want to do?

....

Where did Morwenna work in the past?

....

Why could Morwenna not continue to work there?

....

Could Morwenna buy broad beans?

....

What did Morwenna buy altogether?

....

Why could Morwenna not stop at the surgery?

....

Why would Morwenna not have been able to accept a lift to the surgery the day before?

....

Finally: think of and write down a question that you might ask Morwenna.

....

Practis Ugens
Exercise Twenty

Translate the following passage into Cornish:

Hello John, how are you? I'm fine. We took a summer holiday in Brittany (**Breten Vyhan**). Did you fly? (**neyja**) No, we went ('did go') over the water. What was the food (**boos**) like? Oh, very good. We drank good wine (**gwin**) and ate good food. What did you eat? Oh, we ate French bread (**bara Frynkek**) and mussels (**meskel**) and French cheese and beef ('cow meat'). Did Morwenna enjoy the holiday? ('Was the summer holiday good with Morwenna?') Yes, she danced every night, that was Breton dancing. I have never (**bythqweth**) done Breton dancing. Is it difficult (**cales**)? No, it's not difficult but each dance (**dons**) is long. (**hir**) I cannot dance well. I couldn't dance well, but I can dance well after Brittany!

Note: In Cornish verb "infinitives" are really verbal nouns, and can be used as other nouns are. For example, **cana da** means 'good singing'. So we can say: **Cana yw da genev** 'I like singing'.

Dyscas Pymthek
Lesson Fifteen

Commands in Cornish

In Cornish we have special forms of the verbs that are used to give commands. All verbs have an imperative form, but an easy way to get around learning them all (at least at first!) is to use **gwra** 'do!' in the singular, or **gwrewgh** 'do!' in the plural, in front of the infinitive or verb in its unaltered state. For example:

Gwrewgh ow sewya!	Follow me! (lit. 'Do my following!')
Gwra scrifa dha hanow omma!	Write your name here!
Gwra fistena!	Hurry up!
Gwrewgh esedha!	Sit down!

As well as commanding someone or some people to do something we can tell them not to do it by placing **na** in front of the verbal noun, as **na wra** or **na wrewgh**.

Why not play a game in your group—using verbs that you have learned so far—of telling each other what they must do in Cornish?

Adverbs

Adverbs are words that describe the action of a verb. We have already learned one without knowing it, that is **yn ta**. Therefore we add **yn** to an adjective to make it an adverb, **yn** + **da** (good). **yn**, or the adverbial particle, therefore causes Fifth State mutation. Refer ahead to the chart on page 79 to see what letters are affected. To say 'truly' or 'in truth', we say **yn gwir** in Cornish. Here the **yn** is the preposition meaning 'in', not the adverbial particle **yn** which causes the Fifth State Mutation.

"Trystan, gwra fistena ha
gwisca dha gota."

"Dha gota a vynn
dha witha yn tomm."

"An ki a wra dos genen
yn lowen."

"Gwra dos yn uskis, Bolster."

"Gwra y gerhes, Bolster!"

"Gwra y ry dhymm."
Ev a yll ponya yn ta.

Read and understand the little story above. *New words*: **gwisca** 'to dress', **cota** 'coat', **fistena** 'to hurry', **kerhes** 'to bring, to fetch', **uskis** 'quickly'.

Practis Onen warn ugens
Exercise Twenty-one

Translate the following statements into Cornish, the first one is done for you:

The boys came home happily.
An vebyon a wrug dos tre yn lowen.

The children are running to school.

....

Run quickly (**scav** 'quick') the train is coming!

....

We wanted to go to Wales for the summer holiday (**degolyow hav**).

....

They can sing well.

....

We sang badly.

....

Pull (**tenna**) the rope (**lovan**) using (**owth usya**) your legs strongly!

....

My cat is drinking the milk greedily. (**crefny** 'greedy')

....

I carried the cases (**trogow dillas**) with my strong arms.

....

Sit here under the tree John, we can eat our our picnic lunch (**croust**) quietly (**cosel** 'quiet').

....

I cannot read any longer (**na fella**), my eyes are tired.

....

Children don't run, you will fall (**codha**) and injure (**shyndya**) your knees.

....

I like riding if the weather is good.

....

I like surfing (**mordardha**) if the weather is bad and the waves (**tonnow**) are large.

....

We are walking to school today. Mum says we will have good health (**yehes da**).

....

Dyscas Whetek
Lesson Sixteen

Days of the week:

de Sul	Sunday
de Lun	Monday
de Meurth	Tuesday
de Merher	Wednesday
de Yow	Thursday
de Gwener	Friday
de Sadorn	Saturday

Months of the year:

mis Genver	January
mis Whevrel	February
mis Meurth	March
mis Ebrel	April
mis Me	May
Metheven, mis Efen	June
mis Gortheren	July
mis Est	August
mis Gwynngala	September
mis Hedra	October
mis Du	November
mis Kevardhu	December

Notice that June has two names; the word **mis** is not used with the first, **Metheven**.

Time and Ordinal Numbers

In Lesson Nine of this book we learned how to count up until 39. We learned that 'twenty' was **ugens**. **Ugens** is similar to the English word a 'score'. If we want to say 'forty' we say **dew ugens** 'two score'; 'sixty' is **tri ugens**, and so on. You will remember that up until 39 we say that the numbers are on the score (**warn**), after forty we say 'and two score' etc. **ha dew ugens, ha tri ugens, ha peswar ugens**. The Cornish word for 'one hundred' is **cans**; if we want to say 'fifty' we can say either **deg ha dew ugens**, or **hanter-cans**. We learned ordinal numbers up to ten in Lesson Four, in addition we have further ordinal numbers:

Cardinal numerals		*Ordinal numerals*	
1	**onen**	1[a]	**kensa**
2	**dew, diw**	2nd, 2[a]	**second, nessa**
3	**tri, teyr**	3[a]	**tressa**
4	**peswar, peder**	4[a]	**peswora**
5	**pymp**	5[es]	**pympes**
6	**whegh**	6[ves]	**wheghves**
7	**seyth**	7[ves]	**seythves**
8	**eth**	8[ves]	**ethves**
9	**naw**	9[ves]	**nawves**
10	**deg**	10[ves]	**degves**
11	**unnek**	11[ves]	**unnegves**
12	**dewdhek**	12[ves]	**dewdhegves**
13	**tredhek**	13[ves]	**tredhegves**
14	**peswardhek**	14[ves]	**peswardhegves**
15	**pymthek**	15[ves]	**pymthegves**
16	**whetek**	16[ves]	**whetegves**
17	**seytek**	17[ves]	**seytegves**
18	**etek**	18[ves]	**etegves**
19	**nownjek**	19[ves]	**nownjegves**
20	**ugens**	20[ves]	**ugensves**
30	**deg warn ugens**	30[ves]	**degves warn ugens**
40	**dew ugens**	40[ves]	**dew ugensves**
50	**hanter-cans**	50[ves]	**hanter-cansves**
60	**tri ugens**	60[ves]	**tri ugensves**

70	deg ha tri ugens	70[ves]	degves ha tri ugens
71	unnek ha tri ugens	71[ves]	unnegves ha tri ugens
72	dewdhek ha tri ugens	72[ves]	dewdhegves ha tri ugens
80	peswar ugens	80[ves]	peswar ugensves
90	deg ha peswar ugens	90[ves]	degves ha peswar ugens
91	unnek ha peswar ugens	91[ves]	unnegves ha peswar ugens
92	dewdhek ha peswar ugens	92[ves]	dewdhegves ha peswar ugens
100	cans	100[ves]	cansves
101	cans hag onen	101[a]	kensa ha cans
110	cans ha deg	110[ves]	degves ha cans
120	whegh ugens	120[ves]	whegh ugensves
140	seyth ugens	140[ves]	seyth ugensves
150	cans ha hanter-cans	150[ves]	cans ha hanter-cansves
160	eth ugens	160[ves]	eth ugensves
180	naw ugens	180[ves]	naw ugensves
200	dew cans	200[ves]	dew cansves
1,000	mil	1,000[ves]	milves
1,000,000	milvil, milyon	1,000,000[ves]	milvilves, milyonves

As in other languages, in Cornish the date can be written in long and short forms. For example:

de Lun an tredhegves mis Ebrel 2009
'Monday the thirteenth of April 2009'

Lun, 13 Ebrel 2009
'Monday, 13 April 2009'

Practis Tri warn ugens
Exercise Twenty-three

Write the following dates in Cornish, in long and short forms:

Tuesday 27 January   Thursday 5 March

....

....

Saturday 9 May   Sunday 21 June

....

....

Wednesday 18 November   Friday 25 December

....

....

Seasons

The seasons in Cornish are as follows:

gwav	winter
gwenton	spring
hav	summer
kynnyav	autumn

A week is **seythen** and a year is **bledhen**; a day other than as a prefix for a day of the week is **dedh**.

We have learned the word **lies** 'many'; to ask 'how many' we say **Py lies?**

Practis Peswar warn ugens • *Exercise Twenty-four*

You should now be able to answer questions of the following type, the first one is answered for you:

Py lies dedh eus y'n seythen?   **Yma seyth dedh y'n seythen**

Py lies mis eus y'n vledhen?

....

Py lies dedh eus yn diw seython?

....

Py lies den eus yn para pel droos?

....

Py lies den eus yn para pel droos rugby?

....

"Monday's Child" in Cornish

Flogh an Lun a gav *ponow* **poos,**
ha flogh an Merth fordh *bell* **dhe vos,**
flogh an Merher yw teg y *fas,*
flogh an Yow yw *leun* **a** *ras,*
flogh an Gwener yw *hegar hel,*
flogh an Sadorn *a gav* **meur a** *whel,*
Mes pub flogh *genys* **De Sul** *Duw*
'vydh teg ha lowen, da ha *gwiw.*

Read this aloud and get used to putting a poetical rhythm into the words. No doubt you recognize the original English version! Try to work out the *exact* meaning of the Cornish words.

New words: **a gav** 'gets', **Duw** 'God', **fas** 'face', **genys** 'born', **gras** 'grace', **gwiw** 'deserving', **hegar** 'lovable', **hel** 'generous', **leun** 'full', **para** 'team', **pell** 'far', **ponow** 'woe', **whel** 'work'.

Notes: **dedh** has a special mutation after **an** 'the': **an jedh**. The word **poos** 'heavy' can also mean 'oppressive'.

Dyscas Seytek
Lesson Seventeen

More Prepositional Pronouns

In Part two we learned the Prenominal Prepostions **gans** and **dhe**. In this section we learn two more. The first is for **rag** 'for', and the second is **orth** 'at'.

	Rag		*Orth*
for me	**ragov**	at me	**orthiv**
for thee	**ragos**	at thee	**orthis**
for him	**ragdho**	at him	**orto**
for her	**rygdhy**	at her	**orty**
for us	**ragon**	at us	**orthyn**
for you	**ragowgh**	at you	**orthowgh**
for them	**ragdha**	at them	**orta**

The word **rag** has the sense 'for the purpose of' so, if you were lending someone a bicycle you would say **Ot omma diwros ragos**, but if you were giving someone a bicycle for his or her birthday you would say **Ot omma diwros dhis**.

The word **orth** has a number of meanings in Cornish, it can mean 'at', 'by', 'with' or 'against'. Here are some examples:

My a vynn *pellgowsel* orto.
I will telephone him.

Ev a vynn sevel orthiv yn *dowisyans*.
He will stand against me in the election.

My a vynn sevel orth megy *cigarigow*.
I will refrain from smoking cigarettes.

Gwra esedha orth an voos.
Do sit at the table.

Gwra cowsel orthyn kyns mos.
Do speak to us before going.

Another important word to learn is **der** (also **dre**), this means 'through' or 'by means of'. Therefore we can say:

Y whrug ev ewna an crow dre vorthol.
He fixed the shed using a hammer.

Yma'n gwyns ow *whetha* der ow chi.
The wind is blowing through my house.

Two more important words; **avel** 'like', and **mar** 'as'. This is not the same word as the word **mar** meaning 'if'; **mar** meaning 'as' causes the Second State mutation. Using these words we can make expressions such as:

> **Mar wynn avel an ergh** 'as white as snow'
> **Mar dhu avel an glow** 'as black as coal'

Practis Pymp warn ugens
Exercise Twenty-five

The following is a conversation between two friends while they are waiting for the school bus. Read it and understand it. You can read it aloud with a fellow student as a short play. Remember to put expression into the words.

Lowena   Pandra wrussys gul dres *penn seythen Calan* Me, Jory?

Jory   Wel, my ha tas a wrug mos dhe Wydhyan rag pyskessa. Y whrussyn ny *skynnya* dhe *woles* an als ha'gan *gwelynny* pyskessa genen ha ni a wrug pyskessa dres dew owr.

Lowena   A wrussowgh whi *cachya* tra *vyth*?

Jory   Gwrussyn, y whrussyn cachya dew *vrithel* hag unn *yown*. Y whrussyn crambla bys y'n carr *termyn cot* kyns *morlanow*. Ena, y whrussyn mos tre dhe vamm hag y whrug vy leverel: "Ot omma *puskes* dhis. Y hyllyn cavos an puskes rag *soper*." Lowen o mamm, nyns o res dhedhy prena pitsa yn agan gwerthjy.

Jory   Pandra wrussys jy gul dres an benseythen, Lowena?

Lowena   O, y whrug vy marhogeth war geyn *merhik*, eus dhe gowethes dhymm.

Jory   A ylta jy marhogeth? Nyns esen vy ow codhvos henna!

Lowena   O, gallav. My a yll marhogeth yn ta.

Jory   Yw marhogeth cales?

Lowena   Res yw spena termyn hir ow *tysky* pub tra. Res yw dhis dysky fatel wrewgh whi settya an *diber* ha'n *hernes* y'n *tyller ewn* kyns oll, ha wosa henna res yw dysky kerdhes gans an margh.

Jory   Yw merhik dha gowethes *dov*?

Lowena   Yw, ev yw mar dhov avel *colen* ha da gans *daromres*.

Jory   Esos ta ow mos dhe *glub* scol, Lowena?

Lowena   Nag esov. Esos ta?

Jory   Esov, yth esov vy ow mos dhe'n club *gwydhbol. Synsys*
           hedhyw yw.

Lowena A ylta gwary yn ta, Jory?

Jory   O, y hallav gwary da lowr. Y whrug vy *fetha* ow dyscador.
           Cowlardak yn deg movyans.

Lowena Yma ow thas ow cara gwary gwydhbol, cowlardak yn deg
           movyans, pur dha! He Jory! Ot omma *bar choclat* dhis.

Jory   O, meur ras dhywgh whi, Lowena. Ot omma an kyttrin
           ragon lemmyn.

New words: **bar choclat** 'chocolate bar', **brithel** 'mackerel', **bys** 'until
(**bys yn** is the Cornish way to say 'up to')', **cachya** 'to catch', **Calan**
'first of the month', **club** 'club', **colen** 'puppy', **cot** 'short; especially
for time', **cowlardak** 'checkmate', **crambla** 'climb up', **daromres**
'traffic', **del** 'as (used before verbs only)', **diber** 'saddle', **dov** 'tame',
dysky 'to learn or teach', **ewn** 'correct', **fetha** 'to defeat', **godhvos** 'to
know', **goles** 'bottom', **gwelen** *pl.* **gwelynny** 'rod', **gwydhbol** 'chess',
hernes 'harness', **keyn** 'back', **merhik** 'pony', **mordrik** 'low tide',
morlanow 'high tide, **penn seythen** 'weekend', **pitsa** 'pizza', **pysk** *pl.*
puskes 'fish', **skynnya** 'climb down', **soper** 'supper', **synsys** 'held or
beholden', **termyn** 'time', **tra vyth** 'anything at all, nothing at all',
tyller *pl.* **tyleryow** 'place, position', **yown** 'bass'.

Qwestyons • Questions

Answer the Cornish questions in Cornish and the English questions
in English.

Which Bank Holiday was it?

....

Where did Jory and his dad fish?

....

How long did they fish for?

....

Py par ('what sort') **puskes a wrussons i cachya?**

....

Why was mum pleased?

....

What didn't Jory know that Lowena could do?

....

What did Lowena have to learn first of all?

....

Py par club scol esa Jory ow mos dhodho?

....

In what way did Jory win a game over his teacher?

....

Why did Lowena know that Jory had a good win?

....

Pandra wrug Lowena ry dhe Jory?

....

First	Second	Third	Fourth	Fifth
p-	b-	f-	—	—
b-	v-	—	p-	f-, v-
m-	v-	—	—	f-, v-
f-	(v-)	—	—	—
t-	d-	th-	—	—
d-	dh-	—	t-	t-
ch-	j-	—	—	—
s-	(z-)	—	—	—
ke-	ge-	he-	—	—
ki-	gi-	hi-	—	—
ky-	gy-	hy-	—	—
ca-	ga-	ha-	—	—
co-	go-	ho-	—	—
cu-	gu-	hu-	—	—
qw-	gw-	wh-	—	—
cl-	gl-	—	—	—
cr-	gr-	—	—	—
kn-	gn-	—	—	—
ge-	e-	—	ke-	whe-, we-
gi-	i-	—	ki-	whi-, wi-
gy-	y-	—	ky-	why-, wy-
ga-	a-	—	ca-	wha-, wa-
go-	wo-	—	co-	who-, wo-
gu-	wu-	—	cu-	whu-, wu-
gw-	w-	—	qw-	wh-, w-
gl-	l-	—	cl-	—
gn-	n-	—	—	—
gre-	re-	—	cre-	—
gri-	ri-	—	cri-	—
gry-	ry-	—	cry-	—
gra-	ra-	—	cra-	—
gro-	wro-	—	cro-	whro-, wro-
gru-	wru-	—	cru-	whru-, wru-

Other letters have no mutation.

Summary of causes of Third State mutation:

After the number three either in the masculine or feminine form e.g. **tri thas** 'three fathers', or **teyr hath** 'three cats. It also occurs after the possessive adjectives **ow** 'my', **hy** 'her', and **aga** 'their', e.g. **ow hanstel** 'my basket', **hy fluven** 'her pen', **aga hi** 'their dog', **Na** 'not any', causes Third State mutation in the expressions **na hens** 'not before', **na fella** 'no longer', and **nahen** 'not otherwise'.

Dyscas Etek
Lesson Eighteen

In Lesson Five we learned about a special form of the verb **cara** 'to love' that we use to ask for something. To say that we like or love something or someone we can use impersonal forms of this same verb as follows:

my a gar	I like
ty a gar	thou likest
ev a gar	he likes
hi a gar	she likes
ni a gar	we like
whi a gar	you like
i a gar	they like

nebes is a new word that we need to learn and it means 'a few'. It is opposite to **lies** meaning 'many'. Unlike **lies**, however, when we talk about 'a few' of anything we use the plural form of the following noun. For example:

yma nebes puskes dhodho 'he has a few fishes'

but **yma lies pysk dhodho** 'he has lots of (*or* many) fish'

In Lesson Fifteen we learned how to give commands in Cornish using the verb **gul** 'to do'. Of course other verbs in Cornish also have imperative forms. One we need to learn is the imperative form of the verb **kemeres** 'to take'. This is **kemmer** when used to speak to one person, or **kemerowgh** when speaking politely or to more than one person.

A useful expression meaning 'take care' is **kemmer with** (or in the plural **kemerowgh with**). This can be used as a form of 'farewell' as it is used in English.

Translate the following into English:

Ev a gar y *whor* vyhan.

Hi a gar hy *dama wynn*.

....

....

Peder a gar y gi.

Ni a gar agan *broder* bras.

....

....

Ev a gar y *das gwynn*.

I a gar marhogeth estyl mordardh.

....

....

Translate the following passage:

Yma Peder hag y whor, Morwena, ow mos dhe'n *lyverva*. I a garsa
cavos nebes lyvrow *tochya* an *balyow* coth y'ga *ranndir*. Peder ha
Morwena a gar *whithra* an *jynnjiow*. "Kemmer with!" "Yma'n
lyvrow na ow codha, Peder". Wella a wra aga *hachya*. Yn y dhorn
yma dew lyver da. "Gwra mires, Morwena, Tas-gwynn a garsa an
lyver ma." Y whrons i mos tre gans an dhew lyver.

New words: **bal** *pl.* **balyow** 'mine', **broder** 'brother', **cachya** 'catch',
codha 'fall', **dama wynn** 'grandmother', **gwith** 'protection, care,
guard', **jynnjiow** 'engine houses', **lyverva** 'library', **ranndir** 'district;
area', **tas gwynn** 'grandfather', **tochya** 'touch (**ow tochya** is Cornish
for 'concerning; about')', **whithra** 'search; investigate', **whor** 'sister'.

Leveryans
Pronunciation

The Cornish alphabet has the same 26 letters as the English alphabet.

a, b, c, d, e, f, g, h, i, j, k, l, m, n, o, p, q, r, s, t, u, v, w, x, y, z

There are several schools of thought as to how Cornish ought to be pronounced. The descriptions here are what are recommended by Agan Tavas as representing good, comprehensible, natural, and authentic Cornish. There are some "dialect" options given, based on preferences some speakers have for an "older" dialect and a "later" dialect. Notation in the International Phonetic Alphabet is given below in addition to a plain-text English description.

Vowel length in Cornish

Cornish vowels are either long or short. The Standard Written Form has rules which help to predict vowel length. Some words do not conform to the rules, and these have to be learned separately. Here are the rules:

A. All unstressed vowels are short.

B. Vowels in stressed words of one syllable are long:
    1. at the ends of words, as in **gwra** 'do', **tre** 'homewards', **to** 'roof';
    2. before a voiced consonant, as in **mab** 'son', **dedh** 'day', **kig** 'meat, flesh', **mil** 'thousand', **rom** 'room', **den** 'man', **hir** 'long', **nos** 'night', **hav** 'summer';
    3. before a single **k** in words like **clok** 'cloak'.
    4. before voiceless consonants **gh** and **th**, as **flogh** 'child', in **cath** 'cat';
    5. before the cluster **st** as in **lost** 'tail'.

C. Vowels in stressed words of one syllable are short:
1. before the voiceless consonants **ck**, **p**, and **t**, as in **clock** 'clock', **top** 'top', **hat** 'hat';
2. before consonants written double, like **ff**, **ll**, **rr**, **ss**, as **stoff** 'stuff', **pell** 'far', **carr** 'car', **class** 'category';
3. before a consonant cluster other than **st**, as in **park** 'field', **cans** 'hundred', **porth** 'harbour', **bord** 'table'.

C. Stressed vowels in words with more than one syllable:
1. are usually short;
2. are long in a few words which have to be learned separately.

There are a few exceptions to these rules, generally involving loanwords.

Spellings and the corresponding sounds

a 1a. [æː] when long, the sound can vary from a drawn out version of *a* in southern English *sad* to the *ai*-sound in English *air*: **tas** [tæːz] 'father', **mab** [mæːb] 'son', **cath** [kæːθ] 'cat'.

1b. [æː] when before the voiceless consonants **ck**, **k**, **p**, and **t**, as in **shak** [ʃæːk] 'shakes', **shap** [ʃæːp] 'shape', **plat** [plæːt] 'plate' where the vowel would otherwise be short. Most of these are loanwords.

2a. [æ] when short, like *a* in southern English *cat*: **dall** [dæl] 'blind', **mamm** [mæm]~[mæᵇm] 'mother', **cans** [kæns] 'hundred'.

2b. [ɑ], like *a* in southern English *half*, when short and before **rr**, **rt**, and **lt**: **carr** [kɑɹ] 'blind', **arta** ['ɑɹtə] 'again', **exaltya** [ɛ'gzɑltjə] 'exalt'.

3. [ə] when unstressed it is like *a* in English *sofa*: **scrifa** ['skrɪfə] 'to write', **tavas** ['tævəs] 'tongue'.

4. [æː] or [ɒː] like the sound heard in southern English *laws*, when in spellings which would be long by rule B.2: **bras** [bɹæːz]~[bɹɒːz] 'big', **clav** [klæːv]~[klɒːv] 'sick', **tal** [tæːl]~[tɒːl] 'brow', **als** [ælz]~[ɒlz] 'cliff'.

NOTE: The Standard Written Form permits the words in this last group to be spelled with **oa**: **broas** 'big, large', **cloav** 'sick', **toal** 'brow'.

aw [aʊ] as *ow* in English *cow*: **maw** [maʊ] 'boy', **naw** [naʊ] 'nine', **saw** [saʊ] 'but, except'.

ay 1. [aɪ] as *igh* in English *night*: **bay** [baɪ] 'kiss', **may** [maɪ] 'that', **ha'y** [haɪ] 'and his/her'.

2. [eː] in some words the sound is same as in long **e**, the pure vowel sound of *made* as heard in Wales and Northern England: **bay** [beː]

'bay', **chayr** [tʃeːɹ] 'chair', **payn** [peːn] 'pain', **paynt** [peːnt] 'paint', **gwaynya** ['gweːnjə] 'to win'.

NOTE: The Standard Written Form does not have rules to indicate whether **ay** has the *igh* sound or the *e* sound. Which words are which have to be learned separately.

b   [b] as in English *boy*: **bara** ['bæɾə] 'bread', **brav** [bɹæːv] 'fine'.

c   [s] as in English *s* in *sit* or *c* in English *city*, *certain* before *e*, *y*, and *i*: **cita** ['sɪtə] 'city', **certan** ['sɛɹtən] 'certain'.

ch 1.   [tʃ] as *ch* in *church*: **chi** [tʃiː]~[tʃəɪ] 'house', **chons** [tʃɔːns] 'chance', **chanjya** ['tʃɔndʒjə] 'change'.

ck   [k] as in *ck* in English *tackle*: **clock** [klɔk] 'clock', **luck** [lʊk] 'enough'.

d   [d] as in English *door*: **daras** ['dæɾəs] 'door', **adro** [ə'dɹoː] 'about'.

dh   [ð] as *th* in English *this* or *that* (never as in *thing*): **bloodh** [bloːð]~ [bluːð] 'year of age', **Godhalek** [gɔ'ðælək] 'Irish (language)', **bledhen** ['blɛðən] 'year'. In final position in unstressed syllables, **dh** is pronounced as though it were written **th**: **mynnydh** ['mɪnəθ] 'you will', **prydydh** ['pɹɪdəθ] 'mountain'.

e 1a.   [eː] when long, like the pure vowel sound of *made* as heard in Wales and Northern England: **den** [deːn] 'man', **ger** [geːɹ] 'word'.

   1b.   [eː] like the pure vowel sound of *made* as heard in Wales and Northern England when before the voiceless consonants **ck**, **k**, **p**, and **t**, as in **chek** [tʃeːk] 'cauldron', **stret** [stɹeːt] 'street' where the vowel would otherwise be short.

   2.   [ɛ] when short, as *e* in *bet*: **let** [lɛt] 'hindrance', **kelly** ['kɛli] 'to lose', **genn** [gɛn]~[gɛᵈn] 'wedge', **hemma** ['hɛmə]~['hɛbmə] 'this'.

   3.   [ə] when unstressed, as *e* in English *fallen*: **seythen** ['səɪθən] 'week', **mowes** ['mɔwəs] 'girl'.

eu 1.   [øː] or [eː] when long, as in French *peur* 'fear' or *ö* in German *schön* 'beautiful', or as *a* in English *made*: **leun** [løːn]~[leːn] 'full', **skeul** [skøːl]~[skeːl] 'ladder'.

   2.   [œ] or [ɛ] when short, as in German *Hölle* 'hell' or English *bell*: **skeusen** ['skœzən]~['skɛzən] 'photograph'.

ew [ɛʊ] a sequence of *e* in English *may* and *oo* in *took* in rapid succession: **dew** [dɛʊ] 'two', **bew** [bɛʊ] 'alive', **tew** [tɛʊ] 'fat'.

ey [əɪ] a sequence of *a* in English *sofa* and *ee* in *see* in rapid succession, similar to the way *see* is pronounced in Cockney or Australian English: **seythen** ['səɪθən] 'week', **seyth** [səɪθ] 'seven'.

f [f] as *f* in English *fallen*: **frut** [fɹuːt] 'fruit', **fowt** [foʊt] 'fault'.

NOTE: Initial **f** is often voiced, as in **fenten** (like **venten**) 'spring, fountain', **forgh** (like **vorgh**) 'fork', **folen** (like **volen**) 'page'.

g [g] as *g* in English *get* or *gun* (never as in *George*): **gallos** ['gæləs] 'to be able', **ygery** [ɪ'gɛɾi] 'open', ['ægə] **aga** 'their', **rag** [ræːg] 'for'.

gh [x] or [h]~[ɦ], or nothing, varying from speaker to speaker. Some pronounce it strongly, as *ch* in Scottish *loch*, most pronounce it a bit more weakly, as *h* in *aha!*, while for still others it is silent, as in: **bugh** [biʊx]~[biʊh]~[biʊ] 'cow', **yagh** [jæːx]~[jæːh]~[jæː] 'healthy', **flogh** [floːx]~[floːh]~[floː] 'child'.

gwl as *gl* in English *glass*: **gwlan** [glæːn] 'wool', **gwlascor** ['glæskəɹ] 'kingdom'.

NOTE: Some speakers insert a very short unstressed *uh*-sound between **g** and **l**; imagine saying *"guhlass"* for *glass*. **gwlan** [gʷlæːn], **gwlascor** ['gʷlæskəɹ].

gwr as *gr* in English *ground*: **gwra** [gɹæː] 'does', **gwreg** [gɹeːg] 'wife', **gwrem** [gɹɛm] 'hem'.

NOTE: Some speakers insert a very short unstressed *uh*-sound between **g** and **r**; imagine saying *"guhrround"* for *ground*: **gwra** [gʷɹæː], **gwreg** [gʷɹeːg], **gwrem** [gʷɹɛm].

h [h]~[ɦ] or nothing, varying from speaker to speaker. Some pronounce it *h* in English *hand* or *aha!* It is always sounded in initial position while medially and finally it is silent for some speakers: **hanter** ['hæntəɹ] 'half', **flehes** ['flɛhəz]~['flɛɦəz]~['fleəz] 'children', **crohen** ['kɹɔhən]~['kɹɔɦən]~['kroən] 'skin, leather'.

i	1a.	[iː] in stressed words of one syllable, a long vowel as *ee* in English *seen* or *i* in English *machine*: **gwin** [gwiːn] 'wine', **kig** [kiːg] 'meat', **tir** [tiːɹ] 'land'.

1b. [ɪ] in words of more than one syllable derived from such words, a short vowel as in English *kitchen*: **kiger** ['kɪgəɹ] 'butcher', **tiryow** ['tɪɾjoʊ] 'lands'.

2. [i]~[əɪ] when *y* is stressed at the end of a one-syllable word, it is long as *ee* in English *seen*. Some speakers pronounce it as *ey* (see above): **chi** [tʃiː]~[tʃəɪ] 'house', **hwi** [ʍiː]~[ʍəɪ] 'you (*pl.*)', **ki** [kiː]~[kəɪ] 'dog'.

3. in unstressed position like *i* in English *kitchen* or *satin*. In the Standard Written Form, words may have either *i* or *y* in unstressed syllables (especially in final position), and which vowel belongs to which word must be learned separately.

ia	['iːə] with a stress on the **i**, as *ea* in the name *Lea* or *ia* in the name *Mia*: **bia** ['biːə] 'would be', **fia** ['fiːə] 'run away', **ania** [ə'niːə] 'annoy'.

iw	[iʊ] a sequence of *ee* in English *see* and *oo* in *took* in rapid succession: **liw** [liʊ] 'colour', **piw** [piʊ] 'who'. There is no difference in pronunciation between **iw** and **uw** and **yw**; you have to learn which words use which spelling.

j	as in English *jam*: **jerkyn** ['dʒɛɹkɪn] 'jacket', **jorna** ['dʒɔɹnə] 'day', **jujya** ['dʒʊdʒjə] 'to judge'.

k	[k] always *k* as in English *kitten*: **kelly** ['kɛli] 'to lose', **Kernow** ['kɛɹnoʊ] 'Cornwall'.

NOTE: The sound of *k* as in English *cat*, *kitten*, and *quail* is represented by an alternating set of letters:

  c before consonants and **a, o, u**, as in **cath** 'cat', **coth** 'old', and **cul** 'narrow'.

  k before **e, y, i** and at the end of a word, as in **keth** 'same', **kig** 'meat', **kyst** 'box'.

  q before **w**, as in **qwilkyn** 'frog'.

l	[l] always a "light *l*" as in English *leave*, not a "dark *l*" as in *full*: **lo** [loː] 'spoon', **eglos** ['ɛglʊs] 'church', **gweles** ['gwɛləs] 'see'.

ll	[l] following a short vowel as *ll* in English *tell*: **dall** [dæl] 'blind', **kelly** ['kɛli] 'to lose'.

NOTE: Some people pronounce this as a "light *l*" followed quickly by **h**, or as an unvoiced *l*, less strong than the Welsh *ll*; try putting the tongue in the *l*-position and say **h**: **tyller** ['tɪlʰəɹ]~['tɪl̥əɹ] 'place', **gwella** ['gwɛlʰə]~['gwɛl̥ə] 'best', **pella** ['pɛlʰə]~['pɛl̥ə] 'further, farther.

m [m] as in English *man*: **mis** [miːz] 'month', **kemeres** [kɛ'mɛɾəs] 'take'.

mm either [m] as in English *tram* or *summer* or as [ᵇm] with an unexploded *b* just before the *m*, as in English *webmail*: **tamm** [tæm]~[tæᵇm] 'bit, bite', **omma** ['ɔmə]~['ɔbmə] 'here'.

NOTE: In the Standard Written Form it's permitted to write **bm** in these words: **tabm** 'bit, bite', **obma** 'here'.

n 1. [n] as in English *now*: **nos** [noːz] 'night', **benyn** ['bɛnɪn] 'woman'.
2. [ŋ] as in English *sing* or *sink* before **g** or **k**: **kyng** [kɪŋ(g)] 'king', **yonk** [jɔŋk] 'young'.

nn either [n] as in English *span* or *scanner*, or [ᵈn] with an unexploded *d* just before the *n*, as in English *hadn't*: **rann** [ɹæn]~[ɹæᵈn] 'part', **henna** ['hɛnə]~['hɛdnə] 'this'.

NOTE: In the Standard Written Form it's permitted to write **dn** in these words: **radn** 'part', **hedna** 'this'.

o 1a. [oː] when long, the pure vowel sound of *home* as heard in Wales and Northern England: **nos** [noːz] 'night', **cost** [koːst] 'coast', **don** [doːn] 'carry'.
1b. [oː] when before voiceless consonants or in unstressed position where the vowel would otherwise be short, as in **clok** [kloːk] 'cloak', **cota** [koːtə] 'coat', **costys** [koːstɪz] 'coasts'.
2. [ɔ] when short as *o* in English *top*: **cot** [kɔt] 'short', **toll** [tɔl] 'hole'.
3. [ʊ] when unstressed as the two *o* in English *collaborate*: **gallos** ['gælʊs] 'to be able', **eglos** ['ɛglʊs] 'church', **ebron** ['ɛbɹʊn] 'sky'.

oo [oː] or [uː], a long vowel, as *o* in English *rose* or *oo* in English *cool*: **boos** [boːz]~[buːz] 'food', **bloodh** [bloːð]~[bluːð] 'year(s) of age'. Either pronunciation is acceptable.

ou   [uː], a long vowel, as *oo* in English *cool*: **flour** [fluːɹ] 'flower', [guːn] **goun** 'gown'.

ow 1.   [oʊ] as *oa* in English *boat*: **dowt** [doʊt] 'doubt', **glow** [gloʊ] 'coal'. Note the irregular pronunciation of **cowl** [kaʊl] 'soup' and **cowl** [kɔːl] 'cabbage'.

    2.   [uː] before another vowel it can be pronounced as *oo* in English *cool*: **Kernowek** [kɛɹˈnuːək]~[kɛɹˈnoʊək] 'Cornish language', **lowen** [ˈluːən]~[ˈloʊən] 'happy', **Jowan** [ˈdʒuːən]~[ˈdʒoʊən] 'John'.

oy 1.   [oɪ] as *oy* in English *boy*: **noy** [noɪ] 'nephew', **poyson** [ˈpoɪzʊn] 'poison', [oɪl] **oyl** 'oil'.

    2.   [uɪ] in the two words **oy** [uɪ]~[oɪ] 'egg' and **moy** [muɪ]~[moɪ] 'more', some speakers pronounce this more like English *gooey*.

p   [p] as in English *put*: **peswar** [ˈpɛswɑɹ] 'four', **pymp** [pɪmp] 'five', **clappya** [ˈklæpjə] 'talk'

qw   [kw] as *qu* in English, *quick*: **sqwith** [skwiːθ] 'tired', **qweth** [kweːθ] 'garment'.

qwr   [kɹ] as *cr* in English *crate*: **a qwressa** [ə ˈkɹɛsə] 'if he did', **ow qwrynnya** [oʊ ˈkɹɪnjə]~[oʊ ˈkɹɪdnjə] 'wrestling'.

NOTE: Some speakers insert a very short unstressed *uh*-sound between **c** and **r**; imagine saying *"cuhrrowd"* for *crowd*: **a qwressa** [ə ˈkʷɹɛsə], **ow qwrynnya** [oʊ ˈkʷɹɪnjə]~[oʊ ˈkʷɹɪdnjə].

r 1.   [ɹ] at the beginning and at the end of a word, as well as before and after other consonants, as in Cornish English: **ros** [ɹoːz] 'rose', **dor** [doːɹ] 'earth, ground', **crejy** [ˈkɹɛdʒi] 'to believe'. The final *r* is never dropped as in RP and similar dialects of British English.

    2.   [ɾ] between two vowels it is a single tongue tap, like *tt* in American English *butter* or like the *r* in Spanish *pero*: **cara** [ˈkæɾə] 'to love', **bara** [ˈbæɾə] 'bread', **ygery** [ɪˈkɛɾi] 'to open'.

s 1.   [z] as *z* in English *zeal* in most contexts, especially in stressed words of one syllable, word finally: **tas** [tæːz] 'father', **tesen** [ˈtɛzən] 'cake', **res** [ɹeːz] 'need';

    2.   [z] as *s* in English *Paris* in the plural ending **-ys**: **romys** [ˈrɔmɪz] 'rooms'.

3. [s] as *s* in English *Guinness*, especially in unstressed syllables (but not in plurals): **genes** ['gɛnəs] 'with you (*sing.*)', **gweles** ['gwɛləs] 'to see', **myternes** [mɪ'tɛɹnəs] 'queen'.

4. [s] as *s* in English *mistress*, in the past participle ending -**ys**: **kellys** ['kɛlɪs] 'lost', **budhys** ['bʏðɪs]~['bɪðɪs] 'drowned'.

NOTE: Initial **s** is often voiced, as in **seythen** (like **zeythen**) 'weak', **segh** (like **zegh**) 'dry', **seyth** (like **zeyth**) 'seven'.

sh   [ʃ] as *sh* in English in *ship*: **shoppa** ['ʃɔpə] 'shop', **shugra** ['ʃʊgɹə] 'sugar'

ss   [s] as *ss* in English in *message* or *stress*, between vowels or at the ends of words: **buss** [bʊs] 'bus', **brassa** ['bɹæsə]~['bɹɔsə] 'bigger'.

t   [t] as in English *tall*: **teg** [te:g] 'nice', **myttin** ['mɪtɪn] 'morning', **cot** [kɔt] 'short'.

th   [θ] as *th* in *thin*, *think* (never as in *this*, *that*): **ow thas** [oʊ 'θæ:z] 'my father', **leth** [le:θ] 'milk', **gwitha** ['gwɪθə] 'keep'.

u   1. [u:] or [i:] or when long, as in French *lune* 'moon' or *ü* in German *grün* 'green', or as *ee* in English *see*: **Lun** [ly:n]~[li:n] 'Monday', **tus** [ty:z]~[ti:z] 'people', **fur** [fy:ɹ]~[fi:ɹ] 'wise'.

2. [iʊ] when stressed, at the end of a word, it is pronounced as though it were **yw**, a sequence of *ee* in English *see* and *oo* in *took* in rapid succession: **tu** [tiʊ] 'side', **du** [diʊ] 'black', **Jesu** ['dʒɛziʊ] 'Jesus'.

3. [ʏ] or [ɪ] when short as a short *ü* sound in German *Mütter* 'mothers', or as *i* in English *bit*: **unn** [ʏn]~[ɪᵈn] 'one', **budhy** ['bʏði]~['bɪði] 'to drown', ['ʏdʒə]~['ɪdʒə] **uja** 'to howl'.

4a. [u:] long *oo* sound in English *cool*, same as **ou**: **frut** [fɹu:t] 'fruit', **Stul** [stu:l] 'Epiphany', **duk** [du:k] 'duke', **Luk** [lu:k] 'Luke'.

4b. [ju:] as in English *use* in the word **usya** ['ju:zjə] 'to use'; ['iʊzjə] may be more accurate and was described by Lhuyd.

5. [ʊ] short *oo* sound in English *took*: **jujya** ['dʒʊdʒjə] 'judge', **luck** [lʊk] 'enough', **bush** [bʊʃ] 'bush'.

NOTE: The Standard Written Form does not have rules to indicate whether **u** has the *ü*/*ee* sound or the *oo* sound. Which words are which have to be learned separately.

uw   [iʊ] a sequence of *ee* in English *see* and *oo* in *took* in rapid succession. There is no difference in pronunciation between **iw** and **uw** and **yw**; you have to learn which words use which spelling. Only a few words use **uw**; in this book only **Duw** [diʊ] 'God'.

v   [v] as in English *vine*: **vy** [viː] 'I, me', **gover** ['gɔvəɹ] 'brook', **gwav** [gwæːv]~[gwɒːv] 'winter'. In the word **cavos** ['kæfʊs] it can be pronounced as though it were *f*. In final position in unstressed syllables, **v** is pronounced as though it were written **f**: **genev** ['gɛnəf]~['gɛnə] 'you will', **corev** ['kɔɹəf]~['kɔɹə] 'beer'.

w   [w] as in English *wine*: **war** [wɑɹ] 'on', **war** [wæːɹ] 'beware', **cowethes** [kɔ'wɛθəs] '(girl) friend'.

wh   [ʍ] a voiceless **w**, like the breathy *wh* in accents of English that distinguish *wear* and *where*, such as Scottish and Irish English: **whi** [ʍiː]~[ʍəɪ] 'you (*pl.*)', **wheg** [ʍeːg] 'sweet', **whans** [ʍæns] 'desire'. The sound of **wh** is not [hw] or [xw]. It is closer to the voiceless bilabial fricative [ɸ]; learners who do not have [ʍ] in their dialect may try to approximate the sound of **wheg** as [ɸʷeːg] (like blowing out a candle) or even [fʷeːg].

x   1. [ks] usually *ks* as in English *extreme*: **text** [tɛkst] 'text', **vexya** ['vɛksjə] 'to vex'.
        2. [gz] after an unstressed vowel it may be voiced (*gz* as in *examine*): **exaltya** [ɛg'zɑltjə] 'to exalt'.

y   [j] as a consonant, like *y* in English *yet*: **yeyn** [jəɪn] 'cold', **yonk** ['jɔŋk] 'young', **clappya** ['klæpjə] 'to speak, chat'.

        NOTE: At the beginning of a very few words, before **e**, the **y**-sound is dropped by some speakers: **yeth** [jeːθ]~[eːθ] 'language', **yehes** ['jɛhəs]~['ɛhəs] 'health'.

y   1. [ɪ] as a vowel, in stressed words of one syllable, is short as *i* in *bit*: **gwynn** [gwɪn]~[gwɪᵈn] 'white', **bys** [bɪz] 'until', **bryck** [bɹɪk] 'brick'.
        2. [ɪ] when unstressed, is short *i* as in English *satin*: **kellys** ['kɛlɪs] 'lost', **qwilkyn** ['kwɪlkɪn] 'frog', **termyn** ['tɛɹmɪn] 'time'. In the Standard Written Form, words may have either *i* or *y* in unstressed syllables (especially in final syllables) and which vowel belongs to which word must be learned separately.

3. [i] when final, unstressed as *y* in English *baby*: **kelly** ['kɛli] 'to lose', **ankevy** [æŋ'kɛvi] 'to forget'.

3. [iː] like *ee* in English *seen*, or [eː] like the pure vowel sound of *made* as heard in Wales and Northern England: **bys** [biːz]~[beːz] 'world', **dydh** [diːð]~[deːð] 'day', **pyth** [piːθ]~[peːθ] 'what', **sygh** [siːx]~[seːx] 'dry'. These words may also be written **bes, dedh, peth**, and **segh**. The option is given because some speakers prefer the Middle Cornish [iː] sound and some prefer the Late Cornish [eː] sound. The rule is that you if you prefer to say [diːð] you should write **dydh**, and if you encounter a text written by someone who preferred to write **dedh**, you can still pronounce it [diːð] as you prefer.

yw [iʊ] a sequence of *ee* in English *see* and *oo* in *took* in rapid succession: **byw** [liʊ] 'alive', **pyw** [piʊ] 'to own'. There is no difference in pronunciation between **iw** and **uw** and **yw**; you have to learn which words use which spelling.

z [z] as in English *zeal*: **zebra** ['zɛbɹə] 'zebra'.

Word stress

Stress is not normally indicated in writing. Here, a vertical bar in front of the stressed syllable is used to indicate stress.

In words of more than one syllable the stress falls normally on the last but one, the penultimate. If a syllable is added, the stress moves accordingly, e.g. **'Kernow** 'Cornwall, a Cornishman', **Ker'nowek** 'the Cornish language', **kerno'weger** 'a Cornish speaker', **kernowe'goryon** 'Cornish speakers'.

There are a few words which are irregularly stressed, such as:

Verb-noun endings in -**he**: **yagh'he** 'to heal, get well', **gwak'he** 'to empty', **gwell'he** 'to make better, improve'.

The emphatic personal pronouns: **ma'vy, te'jy, hy'hi, e'ev, ny'ni, why'whi, an'ji**.

Some words have final stress: **a'dro** 'about, around', **yn'wedh** 'also, too', **my'tern** 'king', **a'les** 'abroad', **dhy'worth** 'from', **ha'dre**.

Some words borrowed from English are stressed as in English: **'policy** 'policy', **uni'versita** 'university'.

Gerva
Vocabulary

a¹ *interrogative particle.*
a² *prep.* from, of.
Aberystwyth *m.* Aberystwyth.
adrev *prep.* behind.
adro *adv.* about. **adro dhe**
prepositional phrase about, around.
aga *poss. adj.* their.
agan *poss. adj.* our.
agas *poss. adj.* your (*pl.*).
allas → **gallas** → **gallos**.
allav → **gallav** → **gallos**.
als *m., pl.* **alsyow** cliff.
an *def. art.* the.
Angove *surname.*
arr → **garr**.
ascorn *m., pl.* **eskern** bone.
astel *f., pl.* **estyl** board. **astel omborth**
f., pl. **estyl omborth** see-saw.
av → **mos**.
aval *m., pl.* **avallow** apple.
avel *prep.* like, as.
avorow *adv.* tomorrow.
bal *m., pl.* **balyow** mine.
balores → **palores**.
banallen *f., coll.* **banal** broom (plant).
bar → **par** → **py**.
bara *m.* bread.
beder → **peder** → **peswar**.
bel → **pel**.
bell → **pell**.

benow *adj.* female.
benseythen → **penn seythen**.
benyn *f., pl.* **benenes** woman.
bern *defective verb.* **ny vern** it doesn't
matter, never mind.
bewa *v.* live.
bledhen *f., pl.* **bledhynyow** year.
blomm → **plomm**.
bluven → **pluven**.
Bolster *m. name of dog (and of a
Cornish giant).*
bonkya *v.* knock, hit.
boos *m.* food.
bos *v.* be. **bydh** will be. **esa** he/she was
(*locative*). **esens** they were (*locative*).
eson we are (*locative*). **esens** they
were (*locative*). **esons** they are
(*locative*). **esov** I am (*locative*).
esowgh you (*pl.*) are (*locative*). **eus** is
(*locative indefinite*). **o** was. **on** we are.
os you (*sing.*) are. **owgh** you (*pl.*) are.
usy is (*locative definite*). **yma** is
(*locative positive*). **ymons** they are
(*locative positive*). **yns** they are.
bosty *m., pl.* **bostiow** restaurant. *Cf.*
chi.
bractis → **practis**.
bras *adj.* great, big.
brav *adj.* fine.
bre *f., pl.* **breow** hill.

Breten *f.* Britain.

brithel *m., pl.* **brithyly** mackerel.

broder *m., pl.* **breder** brother.

Brystow *m.* Bristol.

bugh *f., pl.* **buhes** cow.

buss *m., pl.* **bussys** bus, omnibus. *Cf.* kyttrin.

bydh → **bos**.

byhan *adj.* (*also* **bian**) small.

bys[1] *prep.* until.

bys[2] *m., pl.* **bysow** world.

byscadoryon → **pyscadoryon** → **pyscador**.

bythqweth *adv.* never (*in the past*).

cachya *v.* catch.

cador *f., pl.* **cadoryow** chair. **cador hir** sofa.

calan *m.* first day of month.

cales *adj.* hard, difficult.

callav → **gallav** → **gallos**.

calter *f., pl.* **calteryow** kettle.

cana *v.* sing.

cans *cardinal num,* hundred.

canstel *f., pl.* **canstellow** basket.

cansves *ordinal num.* hundredth.

cara *v.* love. **car** he/she loves. **carsa** he/she would like.

cares *f., pl.* **caresow** girlfriend, (female) sweetheart.

carn *m., pl.* **carnow** rock pile, cairn.

carr *m., pl.* **kerry** car, automobile.

carrek *f., pl.* **caregy** rock.

carsa → **cara**.

castel *m., pl.* **castylly** castle.

cath *f., pl.* **cathes** cat.

cavos *v.* get, find.

chi *m., pl.* **treven** house.

chicok *m., pl.* **chicoges** swift, house-martin.

choclat *m., pl.* **choclats** chocolate.

cigarik *m., pl.* **cigarigow** cigarette.

cinema *m.* cinema.

clock *m., pl.* **clockys** clock.

clok *m., pl.* **clokys** cloak.

clor *adj.* mild, gentle.

clowes *v.* hear.

club *m., pl.* **clubbys** club.

codha *v.* fall.

coffy *m.* coffee.

collel *f., pl.* **kellyl** knife.

colya → **golya**.

colen *m., pl.* **kelyn** puppy.

comolek *adj.* cloudy.

corev *m.* ale, beer.

corf *m., pl.* **corfow** body.

corra → **gorra**.

cosca *v.* sleep.

cosel *adj.* quiet, peaceful.

cot *adj.* short.

cota *n., pl.* **cotys** coat.

coth *adj.* old.

cothman *m., pl.* **cothmans** friend, companion.

coweth *m., pl.* **cowetha** companion, fellow.

cowethes *f., pl.* **cowethesow** female companion, girlfriend.

cowl *coll.* cabbage, kale.

cowlardak *m.* checkmate.

cowsel *v.* talk, speak.

crambla *v.* climb.

crefny *adj.* greedy, avaricious.

cresik *m., pl.* **cresigow** potato crisp.

crev *adj.* strong.

crow *m., pl.* **crowyow** shed.

croust *m.* (picnic) lunch.

cul[1] *adj.* thin, narrow.

cul[2] → **gul**.

da *adj.* good. **yn ta** *adv.* well.

dama wynn *m., pl.* **damyow gwynn** grandmother.

dann → **yn dann**.

daras *m., pl.* **darasow** door.

daromres *m.* traffic.

davas *f., pl.* **deves** sheep.

de[1] *adv.* yesterday.

de[2] *prefix used with days of the week.*

dedh *m., pl.* **dedhyow** day. **an jedh** the day.

defendyer *m., pl.* **defendyoryon** rubber, eraser.

deg *cardinal num.* ten.

degol *m., pl.* **degolyow** holiday.

degves *ordinal num.* tenth.

dehen *m.* cream.

del *conj.* as, like.

den *m., pl.* **tus** man, person. *in pl.* people.

der *conj.* through.

derowen *f., coll.* **derow** oak tree.

derrys → **terrys** → **terry**.

desen → **tesen**.

deves → **davas**.

dew *masc. cardinal num.* (**diw** *before feminine nouns*) two.

dewdhegves *ordinal num.* twelfth.

dewdhek *cardinal num.* twelve.

dewlagas → **lagas**.

dha *poss. adj.* your, thy.

dhavas → **davas**.

dhe *prep.* to, for. **dhedha** to them. **dhedhy** to her. **dhis** to you (*sing.*). **dhiso** to you (*emphatic*). **dhodho** to him. **dhymm** to me. **dhymmo** to me (*emphatic*). **dhywgh** to you (*pl.*).

dhe ves *adv.* away. **towlel dhe ves** to throw away.

dhedha, dhedhy → **dhe**.

dhen → **den**.

dherag *prep.* before, in front of.

dhew → **dew**.

dhis, dhiso → **dhe**.

dhiw → **diw** → **dew**.

dhiwros → **diwros**.

dhodho → **dhe**.

dhon → **don**.

dhov → **dov**.

dhu → **du**.

dhymm, dhymmo, dhyn → **dhe**.

dhysky → **dysky**.

dhywgh → **dhe**.

di *adv.* as far as that, thither, to there.

diber *m., pl.* **dibrow** saddle.

dillas *coll.* clothes.

dir → **tir**.

diw → **dew**.

diwar → **garr**.

diwros *f., pl.* **diwrosow** bicycle. *Cf.* **ros**.

doctour *m., pl.* **doctours** doctor.

dohajedh *m.* afternoon.

don *v.* carry, bear.

dons *m., pl.* **donsyow** dance.

donsya *v.* dance.

dorth → **torth**.

dos *v.* come.

dout *m., pl.* **doutys** doubt.

dov *adj.* tame.

dowisyans *m., pl.* **dowisyansow** election.

dowr *m.* water.

dra → **tra**.

dre → **tre**.

dres *prep.* across, past.

drist → **trist**.

dro → **tro**.

drog *adj.* (*usually prefixed*) bad, wicked.

droos → **troos**.

Du *m.* November.

du *adj.* black.

durda dhis *phrase of greeting* God give you (*sing.*) good day.

Duw *m.* God.

dybry *v.* eat.

dyscador *m., pl.* **dyscadoryon** teacher.

dyscadores *f., pl.* **dyscadoresow** teacher.

dyscas *n., pl.* **dyscasow** lesson.

dysky *v.* learn; teach.

Ebrel *m.* April.

edhen *m., pl.* **ydhyn**, **edhnow** bird.

Efen *m.* June.

eglos *f., pl.* **eglosyow** church.

ena *adv.* there, then.

ensampel *m., pl.* **ensamplys** example.

ergh *m.* snow.
erhek *adj.* snowy.
erhy *v.* command, order.
esa → **bos**.
esedha *v.* sit.
esens → **bos**.
eskis *f., pl.* **eskijyow** shoe.
eson, esons, esos, esov, esowgh → **bos**.
Est *m.* August.
etegves *ordinal num.* eighteenth.
etek *cardinal num.* eighteen.
eth *cardinal num.* eight.
ethves *ordinal num.* eighth.
eur *f., pl.* **euryow** hour.
eus → **bos**.
ev *pron.* he, him; it (*m.*).
eva *v.* drink. **ev** he/she drinks.
ewn *adj.* right, correct.
ewna *v.* correct, emend.
fadel → **padel**.
fardellik *m., pl.* **fardeligow** packet.
fas *m., pl.* **fassow** face.
fatel *adv.* how.
fatla *adv.* how.
faven *f., coll.* **fav** bean. **fav ledan** broad beans.
fella → **pella** → **pell**.
fenester *f., pl.* **fenestry** window.
fetha *v.* vanquish, beat.
fistena *v.* hurry, hasten.
flogh *m., pl.* **flehes** child.
flour *m., pl.* **flourys** flower.
fluven → **pluven**.
fordh *f., pl.* **fordhow** road, way.
forgh *f., pl.* **fergh** fork.
fors *m.* matter, care, concern, heed. *in phrase* **na fors** never mind, it doesn't matter.
fos *f., pl.* **fosow** wall.
frank *adj.* free.
Frynkek *adj.* French.
fydh → **bydh**.
fylm *m., pl.* **fylmys** film.

fynn → **mynn** → **mynnes**.
fynnav → **mynnav** → **mynnes**.
fynnons → **mynnons** → **mynnes**.
fynnys → **mynnys** → **mynnes**.
gador → **cador**.
gallos *v.* be able. **gallav** I can. **gyll** he/she can. **gyllens** they were able. **gyllewgh** you (*pl.*) were able. **gyllons** they can. **gyllowgh** you (*pl.*) can. **gyllydh** you (*sing.*) can. **gyllyn** I was able. **gyllyn** we were able. **gyllys** you (*sing.*) were able. **gylta** you (*sing.*) can.
gans *prep.* with. **ganso** with him. **gansa** with them. **genen** with us. **genes** with you (*sing.*). **genev** with me. **genowgh** with you (*pl.*). **gensy** with her.
garr *f., dual* **diwar**, *pl.* **garrow** leg.
garrek → **carrek**.
garsa → **carsa** → **cara**.
gath → **cath**.
gav → **cavos**.
gaver *f., pl.* **gever**, *pl.* **gyfras** goat.
Gembra → **Kembra**.
genen, genes, genev, genowgh, gensy → **gans**.
Genver *m.* January.
genys *verb. adj.* born.
ger *m., pl.* **geryow** word.
gerhes → **kerhes**.
gerva *f., pl.* **gervaow** vocabulary, glossary.
geryow → **ger**.
gewer → **kewer**.
geyn → **keyn**.
glaw *m.* rain.
glawek *adj.* rainy.
glawlen *f., pl.* **glawlennow** umbrella.
glow *m.* coal.
glub → **club**.
glyb *adj.* wet.
godhvos *v.* know.
goles *m., pl.* **golesow** bottom, base.

gonis *v.* work, sow.

goodh *f., pl.* **godhow** goose.

gool *m., pl.* **golyow** sail.

gorow *adj.* male.

gorra *v.* put, send.

gorsedh *f.* meeting of bards.

Gortheren *m.* July.

gorthuher *m.* evening.

gota → **cota**.

goth → **coth**.

gover *m., pl.* **goverow** brook, stream.

gowethes → **cowethes**.

gras *m.* thanks, grace. **meur ras** many thanks.

gromercy! *interj* many thanks!

gul *v.* make, do. **gwra!** do! **gwrama** I do (emphatic). **gwrav** I do. **gwredh** you (sing.) do. **gwreta** you (sing. emphatic) do. **gwren** we do. **gwrewgh**(!) you do; do! (pl.). **gwrons** they do. **gwrug** I did; he/she did. **gwrussowgh** you (pl.) did. **gwrusta** you did (emphatic). **gwrussyn** we did. **gwrussys** you (sing.) did.

gwag *adj.* empty, hungry.

gwandra *v.* wander.

gwary *v.* play.

gwav *m., pl.* **gwavow** winter.

gwaya *v.* move.

gwenton *m.* spring (season).

gwedhen *f., coll.* **gwydh** tree.

gwedren *f., pl.* **gwedrennow** glass, tumbler.

gwel *m.* sight.

gwelen *f., pl.* **gwelynny** rod, stick.

gweles *v.* see.

gwell *compar. adj.* better.

gwelsow *pl.* shears. **gwelsow byhan** scissors.

gwely *n., pl.* **gweliow** bed.

gwelynny → **gwelen**.

Gwener *m.* Friday. **de Gwener** on Friday.

gwertha *v.* sell.

gwerthjy *n., pl.* **gwerthjiow** shop. *Cf.* **chi**.

gweth *comp. adj.* worse.

gwevya *v.* wave (*a hand, etc*).

gwin *m.* wine.

gwir *adj.* true; truth. *in the expression* **yn gwir** in truth, indeed, truly.

gwisca *v.* wear, don.

gwith *m.* protection, care, guard.

gwitha *v.* keep.

gwiw *adj.* worthy.

gwlas *f., pl.* **gwlasow** country, kingdom.

gwra → **gul**.

gwragh *f., pl.* **gwrahas** witch.

gwrama, gwrav → **gul**.

gwredhen *f., coll.* **gwredh**, *pl.* **gwredhyow** root.

gwreg *f., pl.* **gwragedh** wife.

gwren, gwreta, gwrewgh → **gul**.

gwri *m., pl.* **gwriow** seam.

gwrons, gwrug, gwrussons, gwrussowgh, gwrusta, gwrussyn, gwrussys → **gul**.

gwydh → **gwedhen**.

gwydhbol *m.* chess.

Gwydhyan *m.* Gwithian (*place-name*).

gwynn *adj.* white.

Gwynngala *m.* September.

gwyns *m., pl.* **gwynsow** wind.

gwynsek *adj.* windy.

gyll, gyllons, gyllowgh, gyllydh, gyllyn, gyllys, gylsowgh, gylsyn, gylsys, gylta → **gallos**.

gyst → **kyst**.

ha *conj.*(**hag** *before vowels*) and. **ha'gan** and our. **ha'n** and the.

ha'gan → **ha, agan**.

ha'n → **ha, an**.

hag → **ha**.

hallav → **gallav** → **gallos**.

hanaf *m., pl.* **hanafow** cup.

haneth *adv.* tonight.

hanow *m., pl.* **henwyn** name.

hansel *m.* breakfast.

hanstel → **canstel**.

hanter *m.* half.

harr → **carr**.

hath → **cath**.

hav *m.*, *pl.* **havow** summer.

havos → **cavos**.

he! *interj.* hey!

heb *prep.* without.

hedhyw *adv.* today.

Hedra *m.* October.

hegar *adj.* kind.

hel *adj.* generous.

hemma *masc. pron.* this. **hemm** *before* **yw** is *and* **o** was.

henna *masc. pron.* that. **henn** *before* **yw** is *and* **o** was.

hens *m. pl.* **hensyow**, **henjy** way, road, course.

hens'horn *m.* railway.

herdhya *v.* push, thrust.

hernes *m.* harness.

hesken *f.*, *pl.* **heskennow** saw (tool).

hi *pron.* she, her; it (*f.*).

hir *adj.* long.

hoffy → **coffy**.

homma *fem. pron.* this. **homm** *before* **yw** is *and* **o** was.

honna *fem. pron.* that. **honn** *before* **yw** is *and* **o** was.

howlek *adj.* sunny.

hy *poss. adj.* her; its (*f.*).

hyllyn → **gyllyn** → **gallos**.

i *pron.* they.

imach *m.*, *pl.* **imajys** statue, image.

jedh → **dedh**.

jicok → **chicok**.

Jory *m.* Jory, George.

jy *suffixed pron.* you, your (*sing.*).

jynnjy *m.*, *pl.* **jynnjiow** engine house.

jynn tenna *m.*, *pl.* **jynnys tenna** tractor.

Kembra *f.* Wales.

kemeres *v.* take.

keniver *adj.* each, all.

kensa *ordinal num.* first.

kerdhes *v.* walk.

kerhes *v.* fetch.

Kernow[1] *f.* Cornwall.

Kernow[2] *m.*, *pl.* **Kernowyon** Cornishman, Cornish person.

Kernowek *m.* Cornish language.

Kernowyon → **Kernow**[2].

kescows *m.* conversation, dialogue.

keus *m.* cheese.

Kevardhu *m.* December.

kewer *f.* weather.

keyn *m.* back.

ki *m.*, *pl.* **keun** dog.

kig *m.* meat, flesh. **kig on** lamb (*meat*).

kiger *m.*, *pl.* **kigoryon** butcher.

kynnyav *m.* autumn.

kyns *adv.* before.

kyst *f.* box.

kyttrin *m.*, *pl.* **kyttrinyow** bus. *Cf.* **buss**.

lagas *m.*, *dual* **dewlagas**, *pl.* **lagasow** eye.

lawlen → **glawlen**.

ledan *adj.* wide.

lemmel *v.* jump, leap.

lemmyn *adv.* now.

lesk lovan *m.* (children's) swing.

leth *m.* milk.

leun *adj.* full.

leur *m.*, *pl.* **leuryow** floor.

leverel *v.* say, tell.

leveryans *m.* pronunciation.

lies *adj.* many.

linenner *m.*, *pl.* **linenoryon** ruler (*for drawing lines*).

liwans *m.*, *pl.* **liwansow** drawing, picture.

lo *f.*, *pl.* **loyow** spoon.

loder *m.*, *pl.* **lodrow** sock.

logh *m.* inlet, lake.

logosen *f.*, *coll.* **logos** mouse.

loren *f.*, *pl.* **lorennow** satellite.

lost *m.*, *pl.* **lostow** tail.
lostek *m.*, *pl.* **lostogas** fox.
Loundres *m.* London.
lovan *f.*, *pl.* **lovanow** rope.
lowarth *m.*, *pl.* **lowarthow** garden.
lowen *adj.* joyful, happy.
lowena *f.* happiness, joy.
lowr *adv.* enough.
Lun *m.* Monday. **de Lun** on Monday.
lyb → **glyb**.
lyver *m.*, *pl.* **lyvrow** book.
lyverva *f.*, *pl.* **lyvervaow** library.
-ma *suffix used after def. art. and noun* this. **an den-ma** this man.
mamm *f.*, *pl.* **mammow** mother.
mar[1] *conj.* as.
mar[2], **mara** *conj.* (**mars**, **maras** *before vowels*) if.
marchont *m.*, *pl.* **marchons** merchant.
margh *m.*, *pl.* **mergh** horse.
marhogeth *v.* ride.
mars → **mar**.
maw *m.*, *pl.* **mebyon** boy.
Me *m.* May.
medhegneth *m.* medicine, physic.
medhegva *f.* surgery, clinic.
medhek *m.*, *pl.* **medhygyon** doctor.
medhel *adj.* soft.
megy *v.* smoke.
melin *f.*, *pl.* **melinyow** mill.
men *m.*, *pl.* **meyn** stone.
mergh → **margh**.
Merher *m.* Wednesday. **de Merher** on Wednesday.
merhik *m.*, *pl.* **merhigow** pony.
mes *conj.* but.
mesklen *f.*, *coll.* **meskel** mussel.
Mester *m.* Mister.
Mestres *f.* Mrs.
Metheven *m.* June.
metya *v.* meet.
meur *adj.* great. *pron.* much, many.
Meurth[1] *m.* March.

Meurth[2] *m.* Tuesday. **de Meurth** on Tuesday.
meyn → **men**.
mil *cardinal num. f.* thousand.
milves *ordinal num.* thousandth.
milvil *cardinal num. f.* million.
milvilves *ordinal num.* millionth.
milyon *cardinal num. m.* million.
milyonves *ord num.* millionth.
mires *v.* look. **mir!** look! (*sing.*).
mis *m.*, *pl.* **misyow** month. **mis Genver** *m.* January. **mis Hwevrel** *m.* February. **mis Meurth** *m.* March. **mis Ebrel** *m.* April. **mis Me** *m.* May. **mis Efen** (*also* **Metheven**) *m.* June. **mis Gortheren** *m.* July. **mis Est** *m.* August. **mis Gwynngala** *m.* September. **mis Hedra** *m.* October. **mis Du** *m.* November. **mis Kevardhu** *m.* December.
moos *f.*, *pl.* **mosow** table.
mor *m.*, *pl.* **morow** sea.
mordardh *m.* surf.
mordardha *v.* surf.
mordrik *m.* low tide.
morlanow *m.* high tide.
morthol *m.*, *pl.* **mortholow** hammer.
Morwena *f. personal name* Morwenna.
mos *v.* go. **av** I go.
movyans *m.*, *pl.* **movyansow** movement.
mowes *f.*, *pl.* **mowysy** girl.
my *pron.* I, me.
mynnes *v.* wish, will. **mynn** he/she will. **mynna** he/she wished. **mynnen** I wished. **mynnen** we wished. **mynnens** they wished. **mynnes** you (*sing.*) wished. **mynnewgh** you (*pl.*) wished. **mynnons** they will. **mynnowgh** you (*pl.*) will. **mynnydh** you (*sing.*) will. **mynnyn** we will. **mynta** you will (*emphatic*).
mynysen *f.*, *coll.* **mynys** minute.
myttin *m.*, *pl.* **myttinyow** morning.

-na *suffix used after def. art. and noun* that. **an den-na** that man.

na *conj.* (**nag** *before vowels in* **bos** be) not.

na fella → **pella** → **pell**.

nag → **na**.

nahen *adv.* not otherwise.

naw *cardinal num.* nine.

nawves *ordinal num.* ninth.

nepprys *adv.* at some time. *Cf.* **prys**.

nessa *adj.* next; second (*in a series*).

neyja *v.* fly, swim.

ni *pron.* we, us.

nos *f., pl.* **nosow** night.

nownjegves *ordinal num.* nineteenth.

nownjek *cardinal num.* nineteen.

ny *adv.* (**nyns** *before vowels in* **bos** *and* **mos**) not.

nyhewer *adv.* last night.

nyns → **ny**.

o → **bos**.

o! *interj.* oh!

ober *m., pl.* **oberow** work.

ogh! *interj.* oh!

oll *adj.* all.

omborth → **astel**.

omma *adv.* here.

on[1] *m., pl.* **en** lamb.

on[2] → **bos**.

onen *cardinal num.* one. *pronoun* one. *Cf.* **unn**.

orta → **orth**.

orth *prep.* at, by. **orta** at them. **orthis** at you (*sing.*). **orthiv** at me. **orthowgh** at you (*pl.*). **orthyn** at us. **orto** at him. **ori** at her.

os → **bos**.

ostel *f., pl.* **ostelyow** hotel, hostel.

ostya *v.* lodge.

ot omma *interj.* here is.

our *n., pl.* **ourys** hour.

ov → **bos**.

ow[1] *particle used to form the present participle* (**owth** *before vowels*).

ow[2] *poss. adj.* my.

owgh → **bos**.

owr *m.* gold.

owth → **ow**[1].

padel *f., pl.* **padellow** saucepan.

pal *f., pl.* **palyow** shovel, spade.

palores *f., pl.* **paloresow** Cornish chough.

pandra *pron.* what.

par → **py**.

para *m.,* **parys** team.

park *m.,* **parcow** park, field.

part *m., pl.* **partys** share, part.

patata *m., pl.* **patatys** potato.

peber *m., pl.* **peboryon** baker.

peder → **peswar**.

Peder *m.* Peter.

pedrek *adj.* square.

pel *f., pl.* **pelyow** ball. **pel droos** football.

pell *adj.* far. **pella** farther. **na fella** *adv.* no longer.

pellgowsel *v.* telephone, ring, call.

pellwolok *f.* television.

penn seythen *f., pl.* **penn seythennow** weekend.

penntir *m., pl.* **penntiryow** headland.

peswar *cardinal num.* (**peder** *before feminine nouns*) four.

peswardhegves *ordinal num.* fourteenth.

peswardhek *cardinal num.* fourteen.

peswora *ordinal num.* fourth.

pesya *v.* continue.

peuns *m., pl.* **peunsow** pound (money).

pewa → **bewa**.

pitsa *m.* pizza.

piw *pron.* who.

plegya *v.* please. **mar pleg** if you please, please.

plomm *m.* lead.

pluvek *f., pl.* **pluvogow** pillow, cushion.

pluven *f.*, *coll.* **pluv**, *pl.* **pluvennow** feather, pen. **pluven blomm** pencil.

po *conj.* or.

ponkya → **bonkya.**

ponow *pl.* pains, affliction.

pons *m.*, **ponsow** bridge.

ponya *v.* run.

poos *adj.* heavy.

popty *m.*, *pl.* **poptiow** bakery. *Cf.* **chi.**

poran *adv.* exactly.

potya *v.* kick.

practis *m.*, *pl.* **practicyow** practice, exercise.

prena *v.* buy.

prenassa *v.* do the shopping, go shopping.

problem *m.* problem.

prys *m.*, *pl.* **presyow, prejyow** time, meal time, season. *Cf.* **pub.**

pub *adj.* all, every. **pub prys** every time, always.

pur *adv.* very.

puskes → **pysk.**

py? *interrogative pronoun* what? **py par?** what sort of?

pydh → **bydh.**

pymp *cardinal num.* five.

pympes *ordinal num.* fifth.

pymthegves *ordinal num.* fifteenth.

pymthek *cardinal num.* fifteen.

pys → **pysen.**

pyscador *m.*, *pl.* **pyscadoryon** fisherman.

pysen *f.*, *coll.* **pys** pea.

pysk *m.*, *pl.* **puskes** fish.

pyskessa *v.* catch fish.

pyth *pron.* what.

qwandra → **gwandra.**

qwartron *m.*, *pl.* **qwartronys** quarter.

qwary → **gwary.**

qweles → **gweles.**

qwestyon *m.*, *pl.* **qwestyons** question.

qweth *f.*, *pl.* **qwethow** cloth.

qwevya → **gwevya.**

qwilkyn *m.*, *pl.* **qwilkenyow** frog.

qwrav → **gwrav.**

rag *prep.* for, for the purpose of. **ragdha** for them. **ragdho** for him. **ragon** for us. **ragos** for you (*sing.*). **ragov** for me. **ragowgh** for you (*pl.*). **rygdhy** for her.

rann *f.*, *pl.* **rannow** part, share.

ranndir *m.*, *pl.* **ranndiryow** district; area.

ras → **gras.**

re *adv.* too.

redya *v.* read.

redyans *m.*, *pl.* **redyansow** reading.

res *m.* necessity. **res yw dhymm** I must.

revya *v.* row.

rew *m.* frost.

ri *v.* give.

rol *f.* list. **rol an lyver** (*of a book*) the table of contents.

rom *m.*, *pl.* **romys** room.

rond *adj.* round.

ros *f.*, *pl.* **rosow** wheel. *Cf.* **diwros.**

rostel *f.*, *pl.* **rostellow** skateboard (*from* **ros** + **astel**).

rudh *adj.* red.

rugby *m.* rugby (*football*).

ryb *prep.* by, beside.

rygdhy → **rag.**

sad *adj.* serious.

Sadorn *m.* Saturday. **de Sadorn** on Saturday.

safron *m.* saffron.

sagh *m.*, *pl.* **seghyer** bag.

sarf *f.*, *pl.* **syrf** snake, serpent.

saw *adj.* intact, safe.

scath *f.*, *pl.* **scathow** boat.

scav *adj.* light.

scol *f.*, *pl.* **scolyow** school.

scrifa *v.* write.

scubel *f.*, *pl.* **scubellow** broom.

second *ordinal num.* second.

segh *adj.* dry.

selsigen *f.*, *pl.* **selsigennow** *coll.* **selsik** *pl.* **selsigow** sausage.

settya *v.* set.

sevel *v.* stand.

sewya *v.* follow.

seytegves *ordinal num.* seventeenth.

seytek *cardinal num.* seventeen.

seyth *cardinal num.* seven.

seythen *f.*, *pl.* **seythennow** week.

seythves *ord num.* seventh.

shyndya *v.* hurt, injure.

skeusen *f.*, *pl.* **skeusennow** photograph.

skynnya *v.* descend, go down.

soper *m.* supper.

soweth! *interj.* alas!

sqwith *adj.* tired.

stevel *f.*, *pl.* **stevelyow** room, chamber. **stevel esedha** sitting room.

strel *m.*, *pl.* **strelyow** mat.

sugra *m.* sugar.

Sul *m.* Sunday. **de Sul** on Sunday.

synsy *v.* hold, keep. **synsys** held.

syrf → **sarf**.

ta[1] *suffixed pron.* you (*sing.*).

ta[2] → **da**.

talleth → **dalleth**.

Tamsyn *f.* *personal name* Tamsin.

tanbren *m.*, *pl.* **tanbrennyer** (safety) match.

tanow *adj.* thin, narrow.

tanses *m.* bonfire.

tas *m.*, *pl.* **tasow** father. **tas gwynn** *f.*, *pl.* **tasow wynn** grandfather.

tavern *m.*, *pl.* **tavernyow** tavern, public house.

te *m.* tea.

teg *adj.* nice, beautiful.

tejy *suffixed pron.* you (*sing.*).

tenna *v.* draw, pull.

termyn *m.*, *pl.* **termynyow** time.

terry *v.* break. **terrys** broken.

tesen *f.*, *pl.* **tesennow** cake. **tesen safron** saffron cake. **tesen vyhan** bun.

tew *adj.* thick, fat.

teyr → **tri**.

thanses → **tanses**.

thas → **tas**.

thavern → **tavern**.

throos → **troos**.

tiek *m.*, *pl.* **tiogow** farmer.

to *m.*, *pl.* **tohow** roof.

tochya touch. **ow tochya** concerning; about.

tomm *adj.* warm, hot.

tonn *f.*, *pl.* **tonnow** wave.

tonsya → **donsya**.

torth *f.*, *pl.* **torthow** loaf.

towlel *v.* throw.

tra *f.*, *pl.* **taclow** thing (*followed by masculine form of adjective*). **an drana** that thing.

tre *f.*, *pl.* **trevow** farm, town. *adv.* homewards, home.

tredhegves *ordinal num.* thirteenth.

tredhek *cardinal num.* thirteen.

tren *m.*, *pl.* **trenow** train.

tressa *ordinal num.* third.

treth *m.*, *pl.* **trethow** sandy beach, strand.

treys → **troos**.

tri *cardinal num.* (**teyr** *before feminine nouns*) three.

trist *adj.* sad, sorrowful.

tro *f.*, *pl.* **troyow** trip.

trog *m.*, *pl.* **trogow** large box. **trog dillas**, *pl.* **trogow dillas** suitcase.

troos *m.*, *dual* **dewdros**, *pl.* **treys** foot.

Trystan *m.* *personal name* Tristan.

ty *pron.* you (*sing.*).

tybry → **dybry**.

tyby *v.* think, consider.

tykky Duw *m.*, *pl.* **tykkyas Duw** *or* **tykky Duwas** butterfly.

tylda *m.*, *pl.* **tyldys** tent.

tyller *m.*, *pl.* **tyleryow** place.
tyleryow → **tyller**.
ugens *cardinal num.* twenty.
ugensves *ordinal num.* twentieth.
universita *m.* university.
unn *cardinal num.* one (*used before nouns*). *Cf.* **onen**.
unnegves *ordinal num.* eleventh.
unnek *cardinal num.* eleven.
uskis *adj.* swift, quick.
usy → **bos**.
usya *v.* use.
vamm → **mamm**.
vara → **bara**.
varchons → **marchons**.
vebyon → **mebyon** → **maw**.
vedhegva → **medhegva**.
vedhel → **medhel**.
venyn → **benyn**.
vergh → **mergh**.
vern → **bern**.
voos → **moos**.
vorthol → **morthol**.
vos¹ → **bos**.
vos² → **mos**.
vowes → **mowes**.
vras → **bras**.
vre → **bre**.
vrithel → **brithel**.
vy *suffixed pron.* I, me.
vydh → **bydh**.
vyhan → **byhan**.
vynn → **mynn** → **mynnes**.
vynnav → **mynnav** → **mynnes**.
vynnons → **mynnons** → **mynnes**.
vynnowgh → **mynnowgh** → **mynnes**.
vynnydh → **mynnydh** → **mynnes**.
vynta → **mynta** → **mynnes**.
vysytya *v.* visit.
vyth *adj.* any, at all.
wag → **gwag**.
war *prep.* upon, on. **warn** *used with* **ugens** twenty.
warbarth *adv.* together.

warn → **war**.
wedren → **gwedren**.
welen → **gwelen**.
weles → **gweles**.
well! *interj.* well!
Wella *m. personal name* Wella (the Cornish equivalent of Bill, Will, or William).
whegh *cardinal num.* six.
wheghves *ordinal num.* sixth.
whel *m.* work, mine-working.
wherthin *v.* laugh.
whetegves *ordinal num.* sixteenth.
whetek *cardinal num.* sixteen.
wheth → **qweth**.
whetha *v.* blow.
Whevrel *m.* February.
whi *pron.* you (*pl.*).
whithra *v.* search; investigate.
whor *f. pl.* **wherydh** sister.
whra → **gwra** → **gul**.
whrav → **gwrav** → **gul**.
whren → **gwren** → **gul**.
whrug → **gwrug** → **gul**.
whrussyn → **gwrussyn** → **gul**.
witha → **gwitha**.
woja → **wosa**.
woles → **goles**.
woodh → **goodh**.
wosa *prep.* (*also* **woja**) after.
wra → **gwra** → **gul**.
wragh → **gwragh**.
wrewgh → **gwrewgh** → **gul**.
wrug → **gwrug** → **gul**.
wrussons → **gwrussons** → **gul**.
wrussowgh → **gwrussowgh** → **gul**.
wrusta → **gwrusta** → **gul**.
wrussys → **gwrussys** → **gul**.
Wydhyan → **Gwydhyan**.
wynn → **gwynn**.
y¹ *poss. adj.* his; its (*m.*).
y² *verbal particle* (**yth** *before vowels*).
yagh *adj.* healthy.
yehes *m.* health.

yeyn *adj.* cold.

yll → **gyll** → **gallos**.

yllydh → **gyllydh** → **gallos**.

yllys → **gyllys** → **gallos**.

ylsyn → **gylsyn** → **gallos**.

ylta → **gylta** → **gallos**.

yma, ymons → **bos**.

yn[1] *adverbial particle.* **yn ta** well.

yn[2] *prep.* in.

yn mes *adv.* out, outside.

yns → **bos**.

ynwedh *adv.* also, as well.

Yow *m.* Thursday. **de Yow** on Thursday.

yown *m.*, *pl.* **yownes** bass (*fish*).

ytho *adv.* therefore.

yw → **bos**.

Agan Tavas
Our Language

Agan Tavas offers:
- Classes – from complete beginners to advanced level
- Learning materials and course notes
- Correspondence courses
- Opportunities to meet others learning or using the language and to make new friends
- Language activities including plays, storytelling, and treasure hunts and fun activities for young people
- Residential weekends and seminars
- The high quality bilingual magazine *An Gowsva – The Talking Shop*

Agan Tavas Campaigning
- Promoting our national language to all
- Lobbying for greater use of Cornish in our schools and in the media
- Informing national and local government on language issues
- Presenting policy proposals to government departments and requesting action

We are a friendly and welcoming organisation, open to all

www.agantavas.com

Agan Tavas, Gordon Villa, Sunnyvale Road, Portreath, Redruth, Cornwall / Kernow, TR16 4NE, UK

Lightning Source UK Ltd.
Milton Keynes UK
UKOW06f1506230316

270734UK00009B/326/P